Drums, Tomtoms and Rattles

DRUMS, TOMTOMS AND RATTLES

Primitive Percussion Instruments for Modern Use

by

BERNARD S. MASON

Drawings by FREDERIC H. KOCK

❯

46389

DOVER PUBLICATIONS, INC..
NEW YORK

Published in Canada by General Publishing Company, Ltd., 30 Lesmill Road, Don Mills, Toronto, Ontario.

Published in the United Kingdom by Constable and Company, Ltd., 10 Orange Street, London WC 2.

This Dover edition, first published in 1974, is an unabridged republication of the work originally published by A. S. Barnes & Company in 1938.

International Standard Book Number: 0-486-21889-9
Library of Congress Catalog Card Number: 73-90207

Manufactured in the United States of America
Dover Publications, Inc.
180 Varick Street
New York, N.Y. 10014

Table of Contents

Drums, Tomtoms and Rattles

Drums the World Around

MINE is a drum very old. I have many drums—how many I know not without counting them, and each fascinates with the story of the old-time Indian who once claimed it as "his drum". But "my drum" is not to be confused with these—it may be shaped and constructed like the rest and to an observer may seem in no wise more significant, but to me no other could replace it. For the smoky old Indian who gave it to me forbade that any other man should beat it, and his lessons in the use of its potent powers lasted for many days.

My drum is full of memories. Memories not merely of the time-wrinkled Redman and the mingled odors of smoke-tanned buckskin and sweet-grass that pervaded his bark *wakinoogan* in the Pine Land where once it hung, but memories of all ancient and beautiful things of the woods and its people.

My drum is full of mystery, full of Voices. They are heard in its deep rhythmic reverberations, these Voices, and they speak always of olden things, yet in the same breath they seem to speak of youth and more youth to come. They tell of children—millions of them in all the tomorrows, radiant, joyous, dancing—yet they seem to say, these drum Voices, that these same children must know the simple life, the romantic life of the woods; that men will live the modern life better if as children they come to know the ancient way.

My drum tells of lone red paddlers in frail birch-bark canoes, darting down the white-watered streams of the trackless wilderness; of war-canoes of painted warriors gliding across the mirror-magic of turquoise lakes; of lithe, befeathered riders on spotted ponies racing across the Plains; of quiet, soft-spoken

Acoma artists squatted over their silvercraft in the heart of the land of sun, silence and adobe. It speaks of grave and solemn chieftains seated in the circle of council, reverently blowing smoke to the Great One before speaking; of the dreamy, far-off faces of singers as they whip willowy beaters against drums; of the naked painted bodies of dancers, plumes waving in the breeze as their feelings become vibrant in reserved and supple rhythmic movement. My drum speaks of powerful bodies, sinewy muscles, strength, stamina, endurance—of bodies perfectly proportioned and completely developed, sun-tanned and winter-hardened. And of noble, lofty spirits within these bodies!

Yes, my drum is full of dreams—dreams for the future built on a childhood of living with the romantic things of the past.

It is an ancient drum, a sacred drum.

DRUMS THE WORLD AROUND

Drums are universal. There is not a country in the world, or a tribe of primitives on record anywhere that does not make drums of some type or other, and these drums are usually regarded as among the most precious elements of the group's culture. Primitive peoples in particular are inclined to surround their drums with deep significance for reasons that will become clear presently. Drums are everywhere, and the types of drums the world around are many and varied.

Drums mean rhythm—their chief use is to produce a rhythmic repetition of sound. Among some early primitive peoples, a rhythmic sound for dancing was produced without the use of drums; for example, the spectators at the dance would stamp their feet upon the ground, or again the "drummers" would slap the open hand upon some handy object such as a log. Man early discovered that hollow objects produce a louder sound and different type of sound when struck than do solid objects; for example, a hollow log was found to be more resonant than a living tree. The beating of clubs against hollow logs became a very common and far-flung method of producing loud sounds and rhythmic percussions.

While the use of hollow logs as "drums" was wide-spread, it probably reached its highest development among the natives of the islands of New Hebrides in the Pacific, and in other south-sea islands. The New Hebrides tree-drum stands upright, a hollowed-out log placed on end so that it stands up like a dead tree trunk. These logs are frequently huge in size, measuring two feet through at the base and extending into the air from ten to eighteen or more feet. They are hollowed out to a thin shell throughout their entire length except for the extreme top and bottom which remain solid. Down one side there is a long narrow slit perhaps four inches wide extending from near the bottom up to about two-thirds of the length. Immediately above and below the slit is usually found a round hole of about the same width as the slit, and other small holes are often seen near the top. The tree-drums usually taper toward the top with the upper extremity rounded off. Frequently these logs are carved with faces, animals, birds, and geometric designs, executed in a bizarre and distorted fashion which give the poles much the same grotesque appearance that characterizes the totem poles of the Indian tribes of the American Northwest. In New Hebrides a number of these huge resounding logs are often grouped together thus creating the so-called "drum groves" that at a distance look for all the world like groves of dead tree trunks. Each of these logs produces a slightly different

sound from its neighbors, and moreover, different sounds can be produced from any one log by striking it in different places, thus permitting the "drummers" to create many and varied interesting sound effects.

Another type of tree-drum found in the South Seas lies flat on the ground. It is hollowed out to a thin shell except at the ends which remain solid, and has a narrow slit along the top side extending the entire length. Again, there are trough-shaped log-drums consisting of half a log hollowed out to a thin shell with boards inserted in the ends producing an arrangement suggesting 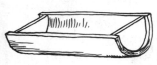 a primitive water trough. Still another type, this to be seen in the Philippines, resembles the tree-drum of New Hebrides except that it is suspended from the branch of a tree and is swung back and forth against a cross-bar made of a heavy pole, thus producing more of a huge bell than a drum—in fact, it is used as a village bell.

These various types of log-drums can be heard for many miles when properly struck by a skillful beater, and they thus constitute one of the chief means of communication, the "language" of the drums being well understood by the natives. Thus the name of *telegraph drums* has often been applied to some of them. In fact, the custom of communication by drum is common in many places other than in the South Sea Islands and is particularly well organized in Africa where an elaborate code of sound and rhythm is developed to carry messages from village to village. Explorers in these parts have often been amazed to

find that their coming was known in villages long before their arrival, and they were mystified as to how this was accomplished until told that the loud-voiced drums had sent the news in all its details reverberating through the woods in code well understood by the dark-skinned natives whose alert ears detected much that the white men never heard.

Hollow logs were not the only objects used by primitives to produce a drum-like sound, baskets being used in this way by some of the Southwest Indian tribes in this country. The baskets were inverted upon the ground and slapped with the open hand. The type of basket usually employed was a shallow, circular one about the size and shape of a mixing bowl, made of roots and grasses woven very tightly and solidly. This same style of basket is used today by the Southwest Indians as a "sounding bowl" for *moraches,* the notched-stick scraping instruments described in Chapter IX. A circle of drummers seated around one of these inverted baskets and slapping it with the open hand can produce a surprisingly loud sound.

Similarly, some Southwest tribes cut a large gourd in half and placing the inverted halves on the ground, beat them with sticks. Sometimes the half gourd is inverted on water and struck.

Now obviously neither the hollow logs of the South Sea Islands nor the resounding baskets or gourds of the Indians can legitimately be called drums. True enough, they produce a drum-like sound and are used for the same purpose for which a drum is used, but if such as these are to be considered drums, then any instrument that resounds when struck is a drum—a bell, a cymbal, a triangle, or even a tin pan or a washbasin. To be a drum, there must be a thin material (usually rawhide) stretched tightly across a frame of some type, in such a way that it produces a resounding sound when struck.

If we limit the word *drum* to instruments of this type, drums are still as old as history and widespread as the wanderings of man upon this old world. Practically all primitive tribes possessed them and they were used and revered by the ancient Egyptians, Romans, Greeks, Chinese, Japanese, and in India.

As one goes from place to place and culture to culture, the drums are found to vary widely in shape and in the materials from which they are fashioned. We find drumframes made of wood, pottery, baskets, metal, gourds, cocoanuts, nutshells, horn, etc. We find drumheads made of the skin of deer, moose, caribou, buffalo, antelope, tigers, lions, leopards, monkeys, elephants, zebras, sharks, cattle, goats, and even human beings, the last-named being found occasionally on ancient African drums. We find barrel-shaped drums, hoop-shaped drums, kettle drums (with rounded bottom), vase-shaped drums, square drums, hour-glass drums (large at each end and small in the middle), egg-shaped drums, etc. We find drums varying in size from tiny affairs made from nutshells covered with skin, up to huge log drums requiring ten men to move them. We find crude drums consisting of nothing more than a hide stretched over a round frame, and again we find drums of elaborate and artistic workmanship made of highly ornamented pottery or of carved wood inlaid with ivory. Drums of all kinds and descriptions—but drums *everywhere!*

No people in the world have made greater use of drums or attached more significance to them than did the tribes of the American Indians. And no drums are more interesting or carry a greater imaginative appeal.

Much of this book is devoted to instructions for making these picturesque Indian tomtoms so full of symbolic meanings and so useful as percussion instruments today.

THE MEDICINE OF DRUMS

Have you ever seen an old Indian sitting alone, absorbed with his drum? If you have, you will appreciate something of the medicine of drums; at least you will agree that to this lone Indian there seems to be a mysterious potency, a spirit power within the drum that in the seeming, at least, transforms him temporarily into a different kind of individual. *Medicine* is an indispensable word in connection with Indian customs, characteristics, and moods—it means *spirit power*. And it is an appropriate word in connection with drums!

As the lone Redman drums away and perhaps sings softly to himself, a dreamy, far-off look comes into his eyes. He seems to become entranced, entirely oblivious to his surroundings, his reverie lifting him above all mundane things. I have frequently witnessed somewhat this same sort of expression, but to a less extent, on the faces of a circle of drummers seated around a big dance-drum and beating rhythm for the dancers.

If the Indian is sad he seems to find solace with his drum. If he is angry his drum brings relief. If he is afraid his drum gives him courage. Whatever the emotion, an hour by himself with his drum seems to compensate and to offer satisfying expression; it gives him a feeling of relief and contentment. An aged Chippewa woman once told me through the interpretation of her son: "I cannot part with my drum. I find so much comfort in it now that I am alone so much."

Drums are precious to practically all primitive peoples. In many tribes they constitute the only musical instrument, and almost universally they are regarded as the most precious of musical instruments. There are several reasons for this:

In the first place, drums mean *rhythm,* and one of the most striking characteristics of primitive men is their response to rhythm. To the rhythmic beating of the tomtoms their bodies react like sounding boards, vibrating with a different emotion each time the rhythm changes. In this respect it must not be assumed that primitive men are any different from the rest of mankind, except perhaps for the unrestrained and uninhibited completeness of their expression, for all men wherever they are found and however complete their development, respond to rhythm whenever it is perceived. In fact there seems to be a universal law of rhythm—we see it in the movement of waves, the undulating of the fields of grain, the swaying of branches of the trees, the rising and falling of tides, in return of night and day, the seasons of the year, the coming and going of years, the beating of the human heart—in fact wherever we look in the physical universe we see rhythmic motion. And man responds to rhythm whenever he senses it, and seeks it when it is not present—*for it is invariably pleasant.* He may merely feel himself in harmony with the rhythm and thus experience it without bodily movement; he may express it in reserved fashion by the tapping of fingers or the beating of time with the foot; or he may exert the whole body as in dancing. But react he will in some way, and experience an elemental joy thereby.

Little wonder that men of all periods have prized drums, the instruments of rhythm, the instruments of *dancing*. All primitive groups loved to dance and the more advanced tribes developed the dancing art to an impressive level of beauty and perfection. No finer example of the expression of life through dancing can be found than the dance-drama of the American Indian. His dancing is his most salient characteristic and the highest form of his art, surpassing his singing, his crafts, and his legendary lore, for all of which he is justly famed. The American public has long recognized the eminence of the Redman's baskets, blankets, pottery, beading, and symbolic design in general, but curiously enough, has not appreciated the fine quality of his chief artistic accomplishment—dancing. Withal, dancing is the Indian's chief source of recreation; of all his forms of play, dancing tops the list. And the drum, therefore, becomes the chief instrument of joy.

Moreover, dancing to the beating of drums fulfilled another community function of unsurpassed importance: It seemed to unite the people, to develop a feeling of group strength and solidarity. Preliminary to battle, for example, long dances were held during which the constant movement to rhythm developed an increased feeling of power, of strength and ecstasy, of capacity to meet any emergency. The drums whipped up morale and flamed esprit-de-corps. (Even today bands play vigorous military marches preliminary to sending soldiers into fighting.) Similarly, the village dances of the Indians in peace times developed an elation, a reckless joy, a high feeling of self-regard, and a sense of harmony with all others in the group. Sociability was increased, friendliness became more pronounced, and all came to feel that the village was a good place and its inhabitants good folk with whom to be. The medicine of dancing drums develops harmony, oneness of feeling and purpose.

It becomes easily understandable from these facts why the council ring or dancing "round-house" was regarded as the center of the northern Woodland Indian village. Even today, no matter how shabby and weather-beaten it may be from the long years of use, it is still pointed to with pride as the focal point of the community. It symbolizes joy, happy days, warmth, friendship, community spirit. And the central object in the round-house is the big dancing drum! Likewise, in the Indian villages of the northeastern woods in the old days there was usually to be seen a big drum supported by permanent poles in the center of the village, uncovered and open to the elements, with·ground packed hard around it from many dancing moccasins. The drum symbolized the community. Whether enclosed in a dancing lodge or in the open circle of the village center, the drum pulsed the heart beat of the tribe.

On a recent visit to the very primitive Chippewa Indian village at Lac le Croix, Canada, I fell in with an Indian who could speak a few words of English and succeeded after repeated requests in inducing him to show us the interior of the old dance house. No sooner had we stepped inside the dilapidated round structure than a wrinkled old lady came running up, filling the air with all the wrath her native tongue could convey. Humbly apologizing, we withdrew and gave her gifts to show our sympathy. Why this objection to our being there? For the same reason that one is not welcome in a Pueblo Indian *kiva*. And this brings us to the most significant aspect of Indian dancing (and of the drum used for dancing)—it means *religious expression*. This was the temple of the Spirit, where the Great One is worshipped through beautiful rhythmic movement—and the old lady was the wife of its custodian!

The effort of the Indian to perfect his dancing, and his intensity in performing it, becomes understandable when we consider that it is his method of expressing religious feeling. The beautiful rhythmic movement, the song and incantation, the bold stagecraft are all to no frivolous end, but in the worship of the One Great Spirit. And the dancing drum therefore takes on deep religious significance. Its mysterious, explosive booming symbolizes the voice of the One Above.

True, there are powwow dances of celebration, there are dances primarily for sociability, there are story dances of exploits, but through them all runs a religious thread. And in addition, there are dances *exclusively* religious, dances seldom seen for they are well shielded from the eyes of curiosity-seeking tourists. And there are various kinds of drums used in these various dances, these drums usually being among the tribe's most holy possessions.

The old medicine man, kneeling over his sick patient, shakes and beats his medicine drum as he vocalizes weirdly with tremulous chants. His is not the sacred *dancing* drum, but still another type—a small hand-drum that has potency in driving out the evil spirit of sickness, and more especially, of filling the patient's spirit with hope, perhaps even ecstasy. And needless to say, these medicine drums vie with the religious dance-drums in sacred regard.

I once asked an old Chippewa Indian who was employed by me to make a certain type of water-drum that I desired to complete my collection. Anger slowly became apparent on his usually stoical face and he finally said, "Must I give you *everything* for the few dollars you pay me? Will you leave me nothing that I can call my own?" No, he did not have to give me everything—this drum was never made.

Often when I have gone into an Indian's humble shack or bark *wakinoogan* to make the acquaintance of its owner and to sit a while, the Indian, after the usual greetings, would promptly point with pride to the drum hanging on the wall or, if it were a big dance-drum, suspended from the ceiling. That he was proud of it was written in every line of his face. On many such an occasion an Indian has attempted to sell me his crafts, but when I pointed to the drum as something I would like, he would emphatically shake his head. Often an Indian will have some drums that can be bought, but in the home of an old-time Indian of the woods or Plains there is pretty sure to be *one* drum that is *not* for sale. Having spotted *this* drum, I have never tried to force a sale. I know of several fine old drums in the homes of Indians at various places in the Northwoods, drums I would like to have, but these I shall never possess, nor shall I attempt to get any one of them, at least not until the old man who prizes it so highly has crossed the Great Divide and no longer needs its ministry.

The medicine of drums is the medicine of dancing, of play, of joy, of art, of philosophy, of religion—of *life*. How can it be all of these things at once? To the Indian these things are all integrated—they are really all one. And the drum is their symbol. And this symbol is full of medicine—*spirit power*.

TYPES OF INDIAN DRUMS

Of all the primitive drums in the world, those of the American Indian are of more immediate interest to the people of the North American continent. They are of more practical value also, in that they are without a superior as rhythm instruments for dancing today. They are of particular interest to dancing teachers, music teachers, physical educators, camp directors, recreational leaders, club leaders, in fact, to all who seek a practical drum that, in addition to its usefulness, provides a delightful atmosphere. There is always a romantic something in an Indian drum, a wild, primitive, woodsy quality that releases imagination. They are good things to have around children. And withal, Indian drums are easy to make. Much of this book, therefore, is devoted to methods of making various types of Indian tomtoms, with the hope that, in addition to their usefulness, there may come the joy derived from the creative experience of making a truly fine and artistically appealing primitive instrument.

Indian drums are of the following general types:

1. *Hand-drums or hoop-drums.*
2. *Large dance-drums.*
3. *Barrel-shaped drums.*
4. *Water-drums.*

1. *Hand-Drums.*—These are very shallow or thin drums in which the hide is stretched over a narrow wooden frame or hoop

three inches or less in width. Such a drum is shown in Figure 9. These are called *war-drums* or *chief's drums* by the Chippewas and Plains Indians because in the old fighting days they were frequently carried by the chiefs on war expeditions. Some of these drums have one head, others two. This same type of drum, equipped with certain rattle devices and painted in certain ways, was used as a medicine drum by the medicine men. There are various sizes and types of these war-drums and hand-sized medicine drums, all of which will be described in Chapter III.

2. *Large Dance-Drums.*—The dance-drums common among the woods-dwelling Indians and to a less extent among the Plains Indians are large instruments suspended between supporting poles, resembling a large wash-tub in shape. Several drummers played them at once. Some of these are called *powwow drums* or *everybody's drums* because they were used for general powwow and similar social-dance purposes, whereas others were surrounded with deep religious significance and used only for sacred rites, as, for example, the Chippewa Dream Dance drum. Chapter IV describes the methods of making these large dance-drums.

3. *Barrel-shaped Drums.*—These drums usually consist of a section of a hollow log with a rawhide drumhead on each end, and are often referred to as barrel drums because they have somewhat the general appearance and proportions of a keg. Figure 66 shows such a drum. They are commonly seen among the Indian tribes of the Southwest. The methods of making these drums are set forth in Chapter V.

4. *Water-Drums.*—Water-drums are among the most interesting of tomtoms. They consist of a waterproof container, either wood or pottery, into which water is placed, and over the top of which the drumhead of skin is stretched. How these drums are made and used is discussed in Chapter VI.

In the discussion of these four types of drums in the chapters that follow, only authentic drums true to the ancient pattern will be described in the sections dealing with true Indian drums, and following such descriptions, instructions will be given for fashioning reasonably accurate imitations from modern materials. It is hoped that the shoddy and cheap affairs sometimes sold at tourist shops in the name of Indian drums will not be confused with the fine instruments these chapters describe. Rather than resort to such as these, it is far better to make a drum ourselves using authentic Indian methods as described in the pages that follow.

PRIMITIVE DRUMS IN THE MODERN WORLD

Myriad are the uses to which Indian drums can be put in the modern recreational-educational program—some leaders and teachers consider them indispensable and all find many unanticipated uses for them. Aside from their utility these drums possess a romantic quality, an imaginative appeal that make them ideal objects to bring into the experience of children. The uses to which primitive drums and rattles can be put are set forth in detail in Chapter VIII; by way of introduction, the following indications will suffice:

Organized Camps.—As a woodsy, primitive craft for camps, drum-making is without a superior. Drums find daily use in camp (1) in providing rhythm for Indian dancing and other types of dancing; (2) in the council-ring ceremonies; (3) in the dining hall as a gong or signal for silence; (4) as a picturesque substitute for the bugle in sounding camp calls; (5) as a means toward educating in rhythm; (6) in rhythm bands.

Gymnasiums.—The modern gymnasium uses drums to provide rhythm for marching, physical movements, and dancing. They serve also as a gong or signal for attention, as a starting signal for races.

Dancing Classes.—The ever-increasing employment of percussion instruments in dancing instruction and recitals indicates the extreme value of the particular types of drums in these chapters. Primitive percussion instruments are not only ideal but indispensable for dancing instruction today.

Music Classes.—In creative music classes in schools and other centers, the making of primitive drums is an outstandingly valuable tool. Drums are needed constantly in such classes to provide rhythm and to educate in rhythms.

Playgrounds and Recreational Groups.—In recreational situations, drums are used to provide rhythm for singing games, children's dancing, marching, and other bodily movements; for rhythm bands; for starting signals for races; and for signals for silence or attention. As a recreational craft, their value is obvious.

Scout Troops, Clubs, etc.—Boy Scout and Girl Scout troops, Camp Fire Girl groups, Woodcraft League tribes, clubs in various associations, churches and settlements, all find Indian drums useful as a means to rhythm for marching and dancing, as a gong for attention, as a starting signal for activities, and as delightful wall decorations.

Orchestras.—Good primitive drums are frequently employed today in large dance orchestras.

The Use of Rattles.—Rattles of the type described in Chapter IX are ideal for use by dancers, by orchestras, and in rhythm bands. As a children's craft they are unexcelled.

The Craft of Drum Making

A WELL-MADE drum with a good tone gives an impression of complexity and skilled craftsmanship that belies the simplicity with which it is constructed. The workmanship on a drum of the primitive pattern may be crude indeed, but if the instrument "works", that is proof sufficient of the skill of its maker. And right here rests one of the chief intrigues of fashioning drums: in the mind of the maker constantly lurks the question, "Will it work?"

One can take particular pains as he goes along in making a tomtom to see that the workmanship is neat and the whole project worthy from the craft standpoint, but neat workmanship does not necessarily mean an instrument that will function as a drum, or if it does function, that it will have a pleasing tone. However expert the craftsmanship, the question still remains, "Will it be a drum, or just look like one?" And when the drum is all complete the question still is not answered—we must hang it up and let it dry for twenty-four hours. As it dries it emits occasional weird, cracking sounds, often loud enough to wake one up from his sleep with the feeling that someone has struck the drum, all of which fills the maker with grave misgivings. But after a full day of patient waiting we apply the drumstick and the drum speaks forth with rich, full tones—*it IS a drum!*

It becomes obvious that there is an element in drum-making not present in most crafts, that of the uncertainty as to the exact outcome. In common with other crafts it involves work with the hands, artistic appreciation, and creativity, all of which bring satisfaction—but in addition to these there is the unpredictable result which adds much interest to the undertaking.

This arises from the fact that the drum really makes itself after the hide is attached to the frame—that is, the wet hide tightens and turns itself into a resounding drumhead as it dries. Perhaps it will be high-pitched, perhaps unpleasantly "tin-panny," perhaps deep and full in tone; through faulty craftsmanship perhaps the hide will be too tight, perhaps it will be too loose, perhaps it will be wrinkled in spots. Who can tell until it has dried?

There is probably no craft in which so large a product can be completed in so short a time. In fact, when one starts to assemble the drum he *must* complete it before stopping—it cannot be done a little at a time. However, granted that all the materials are at hand—the hide and the frame—the actual making of a large drum is a task of no longer than an hour or two.

There will be some who will be interested in drum-making not as a craft but merely as a means to securing good drums for practical use. Dancing teachers, for example, will find Indian tomtoms unexcelled as percussion instruments for use in dancing classes, and since good ones can very seldom be purchased, many such teachers will be interested in making their own. The same will be true of music teachers in schools, physical educators, the directors of summer camps, playground directors, leaders of clubs, Scoutmasters, and the like. Such leaders and teachers will want good drums, large in size and authentic in design, and will be willing to secure the necessary materials.

On the other hand, many organizations will want to install drum-making as a craft for children. Involving as it does the use of woodsy materials and primitive-lore, it is a craft *par excellence* for summer camps. Music classes in schools find in drum-making a particularly appropriate activity. Since drums are inseparably related to dancing, students of the dance usually develop a marked enthusiasm for constructing their own percussion instruments if once exposed to the art. Clubs, Scout troops, and playgrounds can offer no more compelling craft than the fashioning of primitive tomtoms. The craft has been found to appeal strongly to people from seven years of age to maturity.

In contrast to the leader who may want an efficient drum of best materials for teaching purposes, children usually find it necessary to use inexpensive and often improvised materials. And happily such materials are very easy to find. In the following chapters on the craft of making the various types of drums, the plan followed is first to describe in detail the making of an authentic drum by using proper materials, and then to follow with a description of how drums of the type in question may be made from materials that can be picked up almost anywhere. Thus the teacher or leader will not only find instructions for making the best of primitive percussion instruments for his own use, but also ample suggestions for drums well within the reach of all children, however much or little they may want to invest, and whatever their level of skill may be.

There are two parts to a drum, the *drumframe* and the *drumhead*.

MATERIALS FOR DRUMFRAMES

Indian drumframes built just as the Indians make them present a problem that will be described in detail in the various chapters dealing with the different types of tomtoms. We are not limited to the use of these authentic frames, however, for drums can be made out of a huge variety of materials obtainable almost anywhere.

A glance at the following list of possibilities will indicate that no one need want for frame materials:

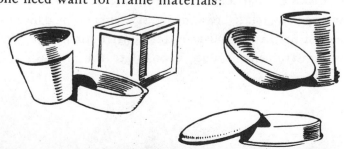

Packing boxes

Barrels

Cider kegs

Nail kegs

Pickle kegs

Wooden buckets

Lard tubs

Wooden wash-tubs

Cheese boxes

Mixing bowls

Chopping bowls

Flower pots

Flower saucers

Number 10 tin cans

Round tobacco cans

Round cardboard cartons

Tin candy boxes

Coffee cans

The methods of using all of these objects will be described in the chapters that follow.

MATERIAL FOR DRUMHEADS

Drumheads are made of rawhide, that is, untanned hide. It is the capacity of rawhide to shrink and tighten when it dries that gives the drumhead the necessary tightness. Tanned hide, lacking this quality, is useless in connection with all except water-drums.

As indicated previously, many kinds of rawhide have been used in making drums in the various tribes and countries around the world, each people utilizing the best they could obtain from the location in which they lived. The woods-dwelling Indians living in country in which deer abounded used deerskin almost exclusively, unless they were making a very large drum requiring a thicker hide, in which case young moose received the call. To the Plains Indians, on the other hand, buffalo calves presented an ever-present source of suitable hide in the old days, while in more recent times, domestic calves offered an excellent substitute. In the far North, caribou hide frequently was used, although the Eskimo preferred the bladder of the walrus and seal. The Southwest Indians, with large herds of sheep and goats near at hand, made excellent drumheads from goatskin. The woods-dwelling Indians maintain that no hide is comparable to deer for drumheads, and they are probably right. Chippewa drums made of deerhide over cedar frames are as a rule decidedly superior to those of their Plains neighbors to the westward, this superiority being due partly to better hide and partly to the superior quality of the white cedar available for the frame.

Deerskin is the choice above all others for drumheads of small or medium size, but of course it can seldom be obtained unless one is located in the Northwoods. Camps in such places can often obtain a deerhide or two from people living in the area who have stored the hides during the hunting season.

Goatskin is the best available material for small drumheads today, and calf skin for large heads. Goatskin is thin, unusually tough and strong, and gives a delightful tone. Drumhead manufacturing companies will provide rawhide (usually calf), suitable for tomtoms of any size, at a reasonable price, but such hide is usually clarified and is nearly white in color, resembling the hide used in band drums and lacking the brown appearance that Indian-made rawhide drums have. Drums made of this clarified skin, while excellent in other respects, do not have the primitive, woodsy atmosphere. This, however, is a matter of taste, and to many will not be a detriment. Some of these companies supply dehaired goatskin especially for tomtom-making, this hide merely having the hair removed and not being processed in any other way. It thus has the appearance of deerhide and when made into a drum is very difficult to tell from a deer drum.

For the making of good serviceable Indian drums of the medium sizes described in Chapters III and V, goat rawhide or thin calf rawhide should be obtained from drumhead manufacturers. The manufacturers will also supply calf rawhide for the large dance-drums described in Chapter IV, if told the circumference of the drum under construction. Such rawhide is not too expensive considering the quality of drum it will produce. Of course, such purchased rawhide is recommended on the assumption that the drum-maker does not care to clean and prepare a fresh hide for the purpose, following the process described later in this chapter.

Sources of Inexpensive Hide for Drumcraft.—Schools, camps, and clubs will find an excellent source of hide for small drums in the scrap pile of broken and discarded drumheads in music stores. Any city music store that repairs musical instruments will have a number of broken heads taken from bass-drums and other band drums which they have reconditioned. Music stores usually keep these and often have a large supply which are customarily sold at such a low figure that the cost is negligible. Among these broken pieces can often be found excellent heads for tomtoms at a price that makes them readily available for children's crafts.

Paper Drumheads.—Two thicknesses of heavy wrapping paper glued together and stretched tightly over the drumframe and tacked to it will produce a makeshift drum that will serve the purpose in a show or pageant, but needless to say will not stand much beating. Another device for throwing together a drum for a show is to tack a piece of cardboard over the drumframe—this makes a drum-like sound.

A more permanent drumhead of paper is made by stretching one heavy thickness of wrapping paper over the drumframe, stretching a piece of thin cheesecloth over the top of it, and then covering both with shellac, thus gluing the cloth to the paper. The cloth gives the drumhead strength and prevents the paper from tearing. The paper and cloth may be tacked or tied to the frame following the general directions for making drums in later chapters, but it cannot be laced.

There is a kind of parchment paper used in cooking called

Patapar which acts very much like rawhide, becoming limp and flexible when wet. and shrinking and tightening when dry. This is so thin, however, that it is useful only on small drums, but it is so inexpensive that it opens the way for drumcraft for smaller children in a very satisfactory manner. It is best attached by binding it to the frame by wrappings of twine. Paper of this type can be purchased at department stores.

Cloth Drumheads.—Good results have been obtained by using airplane cloth as drumheads. When this cloth has been stretched tightly on the frame and then treated with a coat of shellac, or better still, with the special liquid used on such cloth by airplane manufacturers in constructing planes, it remains tight and gives a good sound resembling that obtained from rawhide.

Of the cloth materials more easily obtained, the best are canvas or duck, heavy linen, and the thinner, stronger and lighter substitutes for canvas in tent-making on the order of balloon-silk. These cloths all *shrink and tighten when they become wet* thus acting in directly the opposite fashion from rawhide which shrinks and tightens when it dries. Everyone is familiar with the fact that a tent tightens up in rainy weather—it is this quality of canvas that makes it useful in drum construction. It is thus necessary to stretch and tack the cloth to the frame as tightly as possible and then to wet it thoroughly each time it is to be used as a drum. The water must be thoroughly worked into the cloth by rubbing it with the hands. So soaked, the cloth drumhead gives forth a pleasant drum-like tone, particularly if it is struck gently.

Ordinary canvas is the cheapest and easiest of these materials to obtain, but the thinness, tighter weave, and firmness of the modern substitutes for canvas in fine tent-making make them decidedly preferable for drum construction.

Cloth is best attached to the frame by tacking. For temporary drums, thumb-tacks may be used, and for permanent ones, carpet tacks, or better still, brass-headed tacks, the latter lending a decorative effect.

Rubber Drumheads.—A surprisingly good drumhead may be made by stretching rubber from an old automobile inner-tube over the drumframe and tacking. This gives a good tomtom sound, and needs no tuning as in the case of hide or cloth.

CLEANING AND PREPARING RAWHIDE

Hides secured for drumheads from rawhide manufacturing companies come already cleaned, dehaired, and ready for use. All one needs to do with them is to soak them overnight in water, and they are in shape to place over the drumframe.

There are always some people, however, who are possessed of the true woodcraft spirit to such an extent that they want to perform the whole process of making the drum themselves, even to cleaning the green hide as it comes from the slaughter-house. While not a difficult task this is a rather messy and smelly one, particularly since no chemicals can be used, and those stout-hearted ones whose pioneer spirits urge them to tackle it deserve all praise and cooperation. It should be said, however, that this job should be undertaken only in camps or in the country, and at a point some distance from the campus or living quarters.

Secure a calfskin of the proper size from the slaughter-house on the day the animal is killed if possible; calf is recom-

mended in this case because it will make a good drumhead and is easy to obtain in any community whereas goathides are not so prevalent.

Hide dealers usually throw the hides into brine or other chemical solutions soon after they are removed from the animal, and this may very easily ruin them as drumheads. Occasionally one purchases a cleaned and prepared rawhide from a dependable drumhead manufacturer only to find that when made into a drum it wrinkles badly, has a flat tone, and seems to be burnt. This may be due to the fact that chemicals were used in cleaning it. Drumheads are always better if they have had no contact with chemicals of any type, not even brine, and so we are more certain of success if we can secure the hide soon after it is removed from the animal and before anything has been done to clean or preserve it. In addition to the superiority of untreated hides over treated ones, there is the further angle of atmosphere —the Indians used no chemicals in preparing rawhide, of course, and since we are making an Indian tomtom, it is always better to do the job just as the Indians did it.

If it is impossible to proceed with the cleaning of the hide the next day after securing it, it should be hung up to dry until it is wanted. To do this a frame should be constructed by attaching two horizontal poles to two standing saplings, as illustrated in Figure 1. Small holes are then cut every twelve inches around the edge of the hide and it is suspended in the frame and stretched as Figure 1 illustrates. Heavy wrapping cord may be used for lacings, although the woods-dwelling Indians would use thongs made from the inner bark of basswood, which, by the way, produces unexcelled lacings of great strength. Hides suspended in frames in this way are a common sight near the wigwams and shacks of the Indians of the woods and plains. One often sees deer and bear hides that have been dried and kept hanging in these frames for long periods.

Another method of drying the hide is that of the white pioneer: The hide is merely tacked to the side of a barn. In the Northwoods it is not an uncommon sight to see a half dozen deer-hides nailed to a building, some of them having been kept

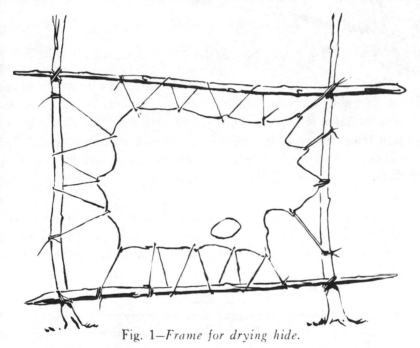

Fig. 1—*Frame for drying hide.*

there for a couple of years. Between the two methods, the frame of poles is much to be preferred.

A hide hung up to dry by either of these methods will lose its unpleasant odor in a couple of days and will remain in good condition for many months even though exposed to the elements. It is usually better, however, to clean it and remove the hair immediately after securing it and before drying it. If this is to be done, place the green hide in a tub of water and let it soak for at least twenty-four hours. In the case of a hide that has been hanging dry for some time, the soaking should continue for about forty-eight hours.

Fig. 2—*Log for scraping hair from the hide.*

Now a log must be prepared on which to scrape it. Secure a log six to eight inches in diameter and about eight feet long. Two legs or supports should be inserted into holes bored about a foot from one end, thus elevating one end of the log while the other rests on the ground, as illustrated in Figure 2. The elevated end of the log should be just high enough to reach the level of the hips.

Next, a scraping tool must be prepared. While an old file may be used for this purpose just as it is, it is better to mount a section of the file in a round stick as shown in Figure 3. The stick should be about eighteen inches long and two inches in

Fig. 3—*Scraping tool.*

diameter. Break off about eight inches of the file, cut a groove in the stick just wide enough so that the file will fit snugly into it and deep enough so that the edge of the file will protrude about one-fourth inch. Round off the ends of the stick to fit the hand, take off the sharp corners of the file, and the scraping tool is ready to use.

Now lay the hide over the elevated end of the scraping log,

hair side up, and standing at the end of the log, proceed to scrape the hair off with the scraping tool. If the hide has been soaked the proper length of time the hair should slip off rather easily and without too much pressure. If it sticks and requires considerable scraping, it should be soaked for another day or two, permitting a little more decay to take place. The scraping should be done evenly and smoothly and without too much pressure because it is very easy to scrape a thin spot into the hide or even to make a small hole.

When the hair has all been removed, turn the hide over and scrape the flesh side, thus removing all fragments of flesh that may still remain. This is called "fleshing." When the underside has been well scraped in this way with the scraping tool, it may be necessary to go over it again with a sharp knife to remove any tenacious fragments that still adhere.

With both sides of the hide properly cleaned it is ready to apply to the drumframe. If the drum is to be made immediately, put the hide in water and keep it wet until placed on the frame. However, if the drum is to be made some time in the future the hide should be suspended in a frame of saplings as shown in Figure 1, and left there until ready for use. A hide should never be left on the ground because worms will quickly attack it and ruin it and the moisture will rot it; furthermore, dogs and many wild animals have a particular fondness for rawhide and are certain to tear it up or run off with it if they can get to it. Neither should the hide be rolled and stored indoors if there is any chance of mice reaching it. The safe place for it is in the frame, suspended as shown.

Indian Hand-Drums

INDIAN hand-drums are shallow or thin tomtoms made over a frame that resembles a hoop. These are light, convenient drums that can be easily held in one hand, leaving the other hand available for manipulating the beater. Their handy size and weight, coupled with the fact that typically they emit a strong, full, and characteristic tomtom sound, make them without question the most practical and popular of primitive drums for ordinary use today. They are ideal percussion instruments for use in dancing, are decorative and ornamental when properly made, and present an unmistakable primitive atmosphere. If well constructed from the right materials, and given the ordinary care that any tomtom should receive, they will give faithful service for many years, and when not in use, will decorate admirably the wall of the den.

Back in the old fighting days when war dances were in order just before going into battle, drums were an essential part of the equipment on all fighting expeditions. Here, hand-drums received the call over the big dance-drums because of their lightness and convenient size—they were no serious burden to carry whether on foot or horseback. It was doubtless this association with fighting expeditions that gave them the name of *war-drums* by which they are known among many northern and Plains Indian tribes. For the same reason one occasionally hears an Indian call them as *chief's drums,* the chief as the head of the war party being the one who usually carried the drum.

Some war-drums or chief's drums have two heads and others one. Very seldom if ever does a single-headed drum appear among the Chippewas, and the mention of such a drum to them will usually bring the remark that that style of drum does not belong to "our people." Their war-drums consist of deerhide stretched over both sides of a hoop. This two-headed hand-drum is characteristic of the woods-dwelling tribes in general. Among the Indians of the western Plains and Northwest Coast, however, a single-headed drum is the more characteristic type, made by stretching a hide over one side of the hoop.

Of these two styles, the two-headed drum is by all odds the better instrument. While the single-head of the Plains performs creditably and is usually a sturdy tomtom, it is not comparable with the other *as a drum.* For resonance, tone, and neat appearance the double-headed war-drum is an easy choice. Of all the hand-drums within my experience, none can compare in quality and workmanship with those of the middle-western Chippewas. Theirs are drums "fit for a Chief."

These Chippewa hand-drums are of two types, the ordinary war-drum and the medicine hand-drum. The medicine drums differ in construction only in the addition of certain rattle devices which will be described in detail presently.

In this chapter we shall consider first the making of authentic Indian hand-drums, that is, drums made just as the Indians made them—this will include the *two-headed Chippewa War-drum,* the *Single-headed Hand-drum* of the Plains, Southwest, and Northwest-coast Indians, the *Square Drum,* and the *Medicine-rattle Hand-drums.* Then we shall take up the making of hand-drums of these types out of materials that can be picked up in any town or city.

TWO-HEADED CHIPPEWA WAR-DRUMS

The most difficult task in making an authentic Indian drum is in fashioning the frame, it being a relatively short and simple task to assemble the drum once the frame and hide are at hand. Later in this chapter we shall see that a number of easily found objects may be used as drumframes, but first we shall consider how the Indians make their war-drum frames, which, by the way, involves quite a feat in woodcraft, but an interesting one, nevertheless.

Making the Drumframe

White cedar or arbor-vitae is the wood above all others for drumframes regardless of the style of the drum. It will make a better drum—no other wood provides a drum of equal resonance; it simplifies the task of drum-making—no other wood combines its lightness, softness, straightness of grain, and bending capacity. It will pay one to go out of his way to secure white cedar rather than rely on other woods, but if it cannot be found, try black ash, basswood, tulip, poplar, or any of the soft woods.

Scout around the cedar swamp until you find a solid, straight, young white cedar, about eight inches in diameter, one with a round trunk free from grooves, irregularities and knots. Cut out of the trunk a section ten feet long that is reasonably uniform in thickness throughout. Split the log in half, then into quarters, and then into eighths. Out of one of these eighths we are to cut the board that is to be bent into the hoop for the drumframe. Better results will be obtained if a piece of wood is selected from the *north side of the tree*—the wood on the south side is inclined to be yellowish as against white on the north side, is more brittle, and more apt to split when being bent into the hoop.

As one looks at the end of one of these eighths it of course has the shape of a piece of pie, as shown in A, Figure 4. The board is to be cut crosswise of this "piece of pie," that is, parallel to the bark edge, as indicated by the dotted lines in C. Split off the pointed section (the triangular section in C), leaving a piece appearing as in D. The width of the top side in D should be about two and a half inches. Now split off from this top side a board one-half inch thick. White cedar splits very easily indeed and the sections will usually come off quite straight and smooth. Three or four good boards can be obtained from each eighth of the log by continuing to split off from the top side of D. Even though only one drum is to be made, it will be well to split off two or three boards in case one should be ruined in bending.

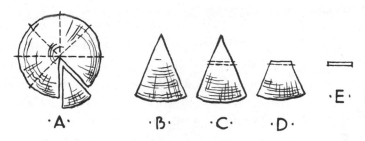

Fig. 4

Now the board must be whittled down to the proper thickness and smoothed up throughout. The thickness depends on the size of the drum desired—a drum under fifteen inches in diameter would require a board one-quarter inch in thickness, and one of larger diameter, three-eighths inch in thickness. The whittling should be done evenly and smoothly, with the grain of the board, and care taken not to make it thinner in some spots than in others, because the board is to be bent into a hoop and if it is not uniform in thickness the hoop will be lopsided rather than circular.

Because of the soft and straight-grained quality of white cedar, the whittling of the board is not as difficult a task as one might assume. A jackknife with a blade at least three inches long should be used. Place the blade flat on the board and take long, sweeping strokes down its length, removing long thin shavings and avoiding deep cuts into the grain.

The Chippewa Indian would do the whittling with a *crooked*

knife of his own construction, shown in the accompanying illustration, which, by the way, is an excellent and most useful woodcraft tool. This he makes from an old piece of steel such as a heavy saw blade. In contrast to the white man's way of whittling, the Indian whittles toward himself with the palm side of the hand *up*.

He grips the knife in his hand, knuckles down and palm side up, and pulls the knife toward his body with long, even strokes. Held in this way with the palm side up, the natural movement is up and away from the board, whereas if held in white man's style with the knuckles up and the strokes away from the body, the tendency is to cut down into the wood and thus to force the knife more deeply into the board than desired. The typical old-time Chippewa is an artist with his crooked knife.

With the board at the proper thickness, we must now reduce it to the proper width and length. The width can vary from one and three-quarters inches to two and a half inches, seldom if ever wider than that unless the drum is a huge one of twenty-four inches in diameter, in which case the width would be three and one-half inches. As a general rule, the narrower the drum the better, and it is safer to err on the side of too narrow a drum rather than too wide a one. Narrow tomtoms have a better sound and are less inclined to wrinkle and become flat and dead in tone. I once heard a very old Chippewa Indian criticising the drums his middle-aged son was making, saying the drums would sound better and last longer if made narrower. The drums of the Plains and Southwestern Indians were usually wider than those of the Woodland tribes.

The length of the board will depend, of course, on the size of the drum desired. The following table will serve as a guide for the dimensions of the board:

Diameter of drum	Length of drum	Width of board
12"	60"	1¾"
15"	70"	1¾"
18"	80"	1¾" to 2¼"
20"	87"	1¾" to 2½"
24"	110"	2" to 3½"

In the table, twenty inches are allowed for overlapping except in the case of the twenty-four-inch drum, where thirty inches are allowed.

The ten-inch section on each end of the board that is to be used for overlapping should be thinned down gradually to about one-eighth inch in thickness at the extreme end.

The board all completed, put it in water and allow it to soak overnight. The best place to accomplish this is in a lake, where it may be laid in shallow water with rocks to hold it.

Bending into the Hoop.—Having thoroughly soaked the board overnight, it will be pliant and can be easily bent into the hoop. Place the wet board over the knee and bend it slightly, then move it along about six inches and bend it again, continuing the process every six inches throughout its length. The board should now have a slight curve. Now repeat this process over and over, bending it more shapely each time, but being careful not to force it too much or it may break. An over-eagerness to complete the task is the surest way to ruin the board—bend it slowly and gradually and soon it will be possible to force it into a circle and thus produce the hoop.

For the best results the *back side* of the board should be on the inside of the hoop. If so placed, the board will bend more evenly and the resulting hoop will keep its shape better than otherwise.

In this bending process the value of good whittling on the board becomes quickly appreciated. If it is too thin in one spot it may break in the bending, or if not, will bend too much at this point and produce a lop-sided hoop.

Overlap the ends about ten inches as in Figure 5, unless it is a big hoop of twenty-four inches in diameter, in which case overlap fifteen inches. Now heat the end of a wire red-hot and burn holes through the overlapped ends as illustrated in A,

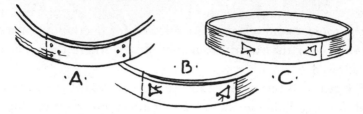

Fig. 5—*Making the hoop drumframe.*

Figure 5—this should be done at two points as shown, near each of the ends. The holes may be made with any small boring tool rather than the hot wire, but the burning is less inclined to split the thin board than is the boring. Now cut off two thin thongs of rawhide from the edge of the hide to be used for the drumhead, soak these well, then run them through the holes and tie as shown in B, Figure 5. When the rawhide thong dries it will tighten and the hoop will be held securely and permanently. Flexible wire used in place of the rawhide will bind the overlapped ends together more securely, but the

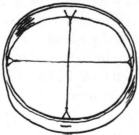

Fig. 6—*Drumframe reinforced by rawhide thongs or wire.*

rawhide will prove amply strong and is the Indian's way of doing it. Furthermore, the rawhide is easily obtained since the drumhead is right at hand.

This completes the drumframe unless it proves to be slightly lopsided, in which case two rawhide thongs or wires attached to the frame and run across it at right angles to each other as in Figure 6, may help to keep it circular as it dries. The thong or wire is attached to the hoop through holes burned through the wood. Strengthening the hoop in this way will usually be unnecessary if the whittling on the board has been carefully done.

A method of producing an absolutely circular drumframe is to slip it over the end of a galvanized can or drum, or other circular object and allow it to remain there for twenty-four hours while it dries. In this case the hoop will have to be made the exact size of the can, which is accomplished by overlapping the ends a little more or less as the conditions demand.

Such methods of making an absolutely round frame are scarcely to be recommended, however, for the very good reason that the drum does not need to be perfectly circular and, in fact, is more attractive if not. Old Indian-made tomtoms seldom are perfectly round. A tomtom is a primitive instrument of the woods and plains, and if slightly irregular it possesses an imaginative appeal, an atmosphere that makes it look the part; perfectly round ones smack of machine-made stuff. Indian projects made by white men so often lack something vital and intrinsic that immediately labels them as un-Indian, and this something is a wild, free, primitive atmosphere, lost through an over-striving for perfect proportion and balance. Let us not be too much concerned, therefore, if the drumframe is not a perfect circle, provided, of course, that it is not too completely lopsided, for, hand-made from woods materials as it is, one could scarcely expect it to be perfect; its irregularities will probably prove one of its chief sources of appeal.

When the drumframe is completed, it should be hung up to dry for twenty-four hours or longer before being used. If covered with hide before dry, it may warp.

If the drumframe proves to be too large for the size of the hide to cover it, it can be easily reduced in size at any time after it has dried. Merely loosen the thongs with which it is tied, force it into a smaller size by overlapping the ends farther, and retie it.

Assembling the Drum

With the drumframe and the hide at hand, we are ready for one of the most interesting experiences to be found in any craft, that of putting the drum together.

The hide should have been submerged in water for twenty-four hours, thus soaking it completely. It is possible to make a dry hide flexible enough by soaking it for an hour in warm water, but much better results will be obtained by leaving it in cold water for a full day.

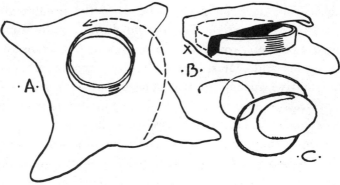

Fig. 7—*Folding the hide over the drumframe.*

Place the hide on a table with the hair side down and the flesh side up. Lay the drumframe on the hide near the neck end, so that the "backbone" of the hide goes directly across the center of the hoop, as in A, Figure 7. The section down the center of the hide that covered the backbone of the animal is thicker and stronger than the rest and if it crosses the drumframe at any place other than the center may cause the drum-head to wrinkle. Now take the tail end of the hide and lay it over the top of the frame, thus covering the frame completely with the hide as in B. (In case the hide is not large enough to cover the two sides, the hoop may be reduced in size, or two hides used, one on each side.) Drive a tack temporarily through the hide at X in B to hold it in place, then proceed to tack the hide to the frame every few inches all the way around on both sides. The tacks should be driven in gently so that they can be easily withdrawn with the fingers. Stretch the hide as you tack so that it is straight and smooth across the drum, yet not so tight that it draws or wrinkles. It is always a problem to know just how tight to stretch the hide, but if it is pulled firmly yet not strained, and when all tacked is spread evenly without wrinkles and apparent tension, so that it vibrates when thumped with the fingers, it is fairly certain to be about right. Most beginners are inclined to stretch the hide tighter than necessary, but happily the drum when all laced and finished, with the tacks withdrawn, has the capacity to adjust itself to the proper tension, unless of course the maker has been unreasonable in pulling it tighter than common sense would dictate.

At intervals of every few minutes while making the drum, the rawhide should be moistened by throwing water on it with the hand and spreading it. Do not submerge the drum in water, however, because that would wet the frame unnecessarily.

When tacked there will be considerable hide left around the edges, particularly of the leg sections. Cut off one of the largest of these sections, being careful not to cut closer to the hoop than an inch and a half. Now, with a pair of scissors cut this piece into a long thong or lacing by going around and around it as indicated in C, Figure 7. The thong should be from one-quarter to three-eighths of an inch wide depending upon the thickness of the hide—it should be as narrow as possible and still be strong enough to stand a gentle pulling. Two thongs are necessary, each long enough to go completely around the drumframe with a foot to spare. When the thongs are all cut, stretch them gently with the hands to see if there are weak places—it is better to have them break before being assembled into the drum than afterward. In case the thong breaks just go ahead and use the short sections and when the end is reached tie the broken end to it. Place all lacings not being used in water until needed.

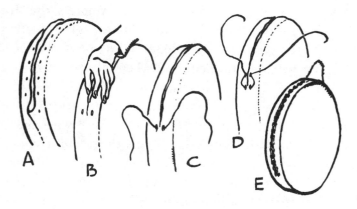

Fig. 8—*Lacing the two drumheads together.*

Since the hide is wrapped around the hoop so as to cover both sides, there is one edge of the hoop that is covered smoothly and tightly by the hide, as shown in B, Figure 7. Start the lacing at one end of this section, at the point where the hide begins to loosen and can be pinched together with the fingers—this point is indicated in A, Figure 8. Pinch the hide together between the thumb and forefinger, and with a sharp knife cut a small hole a quarter of an inch long next to the end of the forefinger, and another next to the end of the thumb, as shown in B, Figure 8. Through these holes run the thong as shown in C, Figure 8, and pull it through so that the two ends are exactly equal. Now about three-quarters of an inch farther along pinch the loose hide together again with the thumb and forefinger and cut two more holes in the same way. Run one of the thongs through these two holes and then run the other thong through the same two holes from the opposite direction, as diagramed in D, Figure 8. Pull the thongs tightly, thus drawing the drumheads together. Now cut two more holes three-quarters of an inch farther along, and run the laces through in the same way, continuing thus until half way around the drum. The tacks are removed as the lacing progresses. Each time the laces are run through the holes they should be pulled gently to make tight. If the holes for the lacings are cut near the edge of the frame the drumheads will, of course, be stretched much tighter than if the holes are placed close together; the holes will be just the right distance apart for a successful drumhead if the habit is formed of pinching the hide together with the thumb and forefinger, and cutting the holes right next to the fingernail and thumbnail.

When the lacing has been carried half way around the drum, start at the bottom again and lace up the other side in the same way. When the two sets of thongs meet at the top and the lacing is all completed, we are ready to tighten the thongs and tie them. Begin at the bottom of the drum, the point where the lacing was first started, and stretch the thongs at each hole tightly. Continue this all the way around until the end of these thongs is reached, and then tighten the other side in the same way. The tightening completed, tie the thongs coming from one direction to the corresponding thongs coming from the opposite direction and the drumheads are completed.

Remember that the hide must be moistened every few minutes as we go along.

Now take a sharp pair of scissors and trim off the surplus

hide that protrudes around the edges. This should be taken off about a quarter of an inch from the lacing.

The next task is to make a handle for the drum. Cut three thongs each a quarter of an inch wide and ten inches long. Braid these together with ordinary braiding, leaving the strands loose for a distance of about two inches at each end for tying. The handle should be tied to the rim of the drum directly opposite the unlaced section. Run one of the thongs under the lacings at the edge of the drum, and another end under the same lacings from the opposite direction. Place the third end of the braiding between these two ends and tie the two ends together tightly. Then tie the other end of the braided handle in the same way and the handle is completed, as shown in Figure 9.

Fig. 9—*The Double-headed Hand-drum with Chippewa design.*

The drum is now completed except for the decorations, which, of course, are particularly important for an attractive Indian drum and are best applied immediately after the drum is completed and before the hide is allowed to dry. The methods of decorating the war-drum both while the hide is wet and after it has dried, together with a number of authentic war-drum designs, are discussed later in this chapter under the heading, "Drum Decorations" (page 78).

Drying the Drum.—With the drum completed the temptation to beat it is almost uncontrollable, but to do this before the drum has dried is the surest way to ruin it. *The drum must not be struck with a beater or even tapped hard with the fingers for a period of at least twenty-four hours after it is completed.* Furthermore, the drum must be dried *slowly and evenly*—to dry it too rapidly will probably result in a warped frame, or in a wrinkled drumhead or one with a dead sound. It can be dried outdoors provided it is hung in the shade on a day when there is very little or no wind. Either the direct rays of the sun or the wind will dry it too rapidly; wind is more drying than sunshine. It is better to hang the drum inside in a reasonably warm place where the temperature will be about constant day and night. If the weather is damp a slow fire should be built in the room but the drum should be placed across the room from the radiator, stove, or fireplace. As the drum dries it will emit cracking sounds, and at times a characteristic drum sound loud enough so that it seems as though the drum must have been struck. This is due to the fact that the hide is shrinking and slipping over the frame. A finished drum frequently makes the same type of sound when the temperature changes.

After twenty-four hours the drum should be completely dry and ready for use. From then on you can thump it to your heart's content.

Another Method of Lacing.—The method of lacing described above is characteristic of the Chippewa hand-drums over wide areas of the Chippewa country. There is another method, however, often seen among the Minnesota Chippewas which results in a slightly neater edge to the drum, yet is not quite as certain to produce a drumhead with the proper tension when prepared by an inexperienced drum-maker.

After the hide has been folded over the drumframe, stretched and tacked temporarily as described on page 45, trim off all the surplus hide with a pair of scissors so close that when the two remaining edges are laid flat on the side of the frame they do not quite touch but are separated from each other about a quarter of an inch. Cut a thong not over one-quarter of an inch wide, long enough to go all the way around the edge of the frame. Stretch this lacing gently with the hands and roll it in the palm of the hand to turn it into a string-like thong

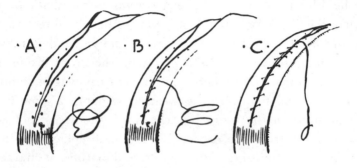

Fig. 10—*Another method of lacing.*

rather than a flat one. Starting at the bottom of the drum, where the hide first splits, cut a small hole just large enough to run the thong through as shown in A, Figure 10, this hole being a quarter of an inch from the edge of the hide. Run one end of the thong through the hole and tie it firmly as shown in A. Then cut a hole through the opposite hide about a quarter of an inch farther along and run the thong through this as shown in B. Continue the lacing in this way as the drawing indicates. The holes on each side are a half inch apart and made no larger than necessary to run the thong through. When the thong is stretched tightly it gives the drum edge the neat appearance shown in C.

Between this method of lacing and the other, the first method is recommended particularly for the novice in drum-making.

While it may leave more hide protruding around the edges of the drum, it nevertheless is stronger and more enduring, and is more certain to produce drumheads that have and will retain, under heavy use, a delightful, reverberating tone.

The Tone of the Drum.—Several factors enter into determining the tone of the drum. Very thin rawhide tends to produce a high-pitched drum without much carrying power but pleasing in tone nevertheless, whereas thick, heavy drumheads are inclined to be low-pitched with deep, mysterious reverberations. Each hand-made drum will naturally have characteristics of its own and happily so, for it is the temperamental nature and the individual traits of primitive drums that make them so interesting and cause people to want to possess more and more of them.

Whatever the pitch of the drum may be, its tone is certain to be reasonably pleasant to the ear if the drum has been properly made, harsh and unpleasant tones usually being the result of faulty stretching of the hide. A very high-pitched drum that emits a short, sudden "pink" when it is struck, without the characteristic reverberations, obviously has a drumhead that has been stretched too tightly. On the other hand, if the sound is dull, flat, and much like one would obtain by striking a beater against a board, the cause probably rests in the fact that the hide has not been stretched tightly enough. If the latter is the case the drum may be tightened temporarily by warming it each time it is used, following the instructions given in Chapter VIII, "Using the Primitive Drum." Neither of these conditions are apt to result, however, if the instructions given in the preceding pages have been carefully followed. But in case they do, we shall have at least gained the necessary experience to get better results in remaking the drum or in making the next one.

Instructions for tuning the drum are given in Chapter VIII.

Drumsticks for Hand-drums.—Hand-drums call for hard beaters of the type described under the heading "Hard Drumsticks" in Chapter VII.

The Tacked War-Drum

By tacking the hide to the drumframe a drum can be made in one-tenth of the time required for lacing it, and the result will be a good drum so far as tone goes, but it will lack the ancient, primitive appearance. Tacks are modern, "civilized" gadgets which are quite generally avoided by the old-timers and, even though sometimes used on drums by present-day Indians, seem immediately to stamp the article as modern and unauthentic in type.

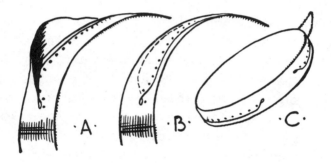

Fig. 11—*Making a tacked drum.*

To make such a drum, fold the hide over the hoop and tack it temporarily just as described for making the laced drum on page 45—since much depends on how tightly the hide is to be stretched, these instructions should be carefully followed. Start the permanent tacking at the point where the hide begins to loosen and fold up, that is, at one end of the section where the hide covers the side of the frame smoothly and tightly as shown in A, Figure 11. The hide at this point should be slit down to where it is tight and needs no tacking as indicated in A. Stretch the hide from one of the drumheads over the frame and tack it along the far edge, placing the tacks about a half inch from this edge, as in A. As will be noted in the illustration the hide at the bottom is not long enough to reach the far side and must be run over to it at an angle. Continue this tacking all the way around the drum, placing the tacks at intervals of an inch and a half.

Now stretch the hide from the other drumhead over the top of this tacking, and tack it in the same way along the far side, as shown in B, Figure 11. There are thus two rows of tacks around the drumframe but only one of these is visible.

If an ornamental effect is wanted the brass-headed tacks so popular among present-day Indians in some parts may be used, whereas if it is desired to make the tacking as inconspicuous as possible, tiny tacks with very small, black heads should be selected.

The fact that tacks have been used in the drum may be completely concealed by covering the edge of the drum with a strip of fur or felt as described later in this chapter under the heading, "Drum Decorations."

To make the handle for a tacked tomtom, cut a strip of rawhide eight inches long and three-eighths inches wide, and tack each end of it to the drumframe at points four inches apart, thus making a small loop for the fingers as shown in Figure 11.

THE SINGLE-HEADED HAND-DRUM

Among the far-flung tribes of the Western Plains, Northwest Coast, and Alaska, the single-headed hand-drum of the type shown in Figure 12 is much more common than the double-headed drums described in the preceding pages. Such drums are also prevalent among the tribes of the southwest mesa and desert country. While these single drums are scarcely the equal of the two-headed Chippewa war-drums, they nevertheless are excellent tomtoms, are easier to make, and use less hide which item is often an important consideration. Frequently a single-headed drum is the only choice because the hide is often too small to cover both sides of the frame constructed to the desired dimensions. In such cases the hoop could of course be reduced in size to fit the hide, but if a large drum is wanted, it is better merely to cover one side.

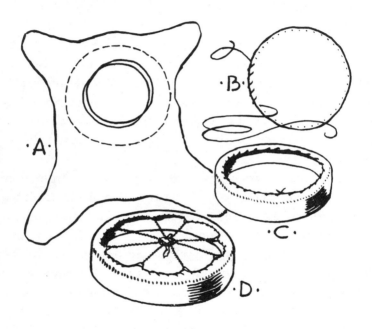

Fig. 12—*Making the Single-headed Hand-drum.*

The hoop for the frame is made just as described for the Chippewa war-drum on page 38, and should be a substantial one to prevent warping, the board being preferably between a quarter and three-eighths of an inch in thickness. While the frame can be of any size, yet the best results will be obtained if the single-headed drum is not over eighteen inches in diameter.

There are two main methods of applying the hide to the frame. Let us consider the more elaborate of these first and then take up the simpler method.

Place the drumframe on the center of the hide so that the "backbone" (the section of the hide that covered the backbone of the animal) goes directly across the middle of it, and then mark the circumference of the frame on the hide by running a pencil around it. Now measure the width of the drumframe (which should be around two inches), add an inch and a half to this and then draw another circle on the hide this distance out from the first one, as indicated by the dotted line in A, Figure 12. Cut the hide along this outer circle, thus producing a circular drumhead large enough to cover one side of the drumframe, fold over its edges and extend an inch and a half over onto the back side.

A row of holes must now be cut around the edge of this circular piece of hide, the holes being slits one-quarter inch long cut parallel to the edge, one-half inch from it, and spaced one inch apart. These holes are shown in B, Figure 12. From the trimmings of the rawhide, cut a long thong three-eighths inch wide and long enough to go around the edge of the drum, following the same process described on page 45, and illustrated in C, Figure 7. Run this lacing through the holes as indicated in B, Figure 12.

Now place the hide over the drumframe, hair side out and flesh side toward the frame; draw it over the sides of the hoop and force the laced edge over onto the back side, as shown in C, Figure 12, which illustrates the appearance of the back side. The head is stretched by pulling on it with the fingers and tightening up the lacing around the edge of the hide: go around and around it, pulling the lacing at each hole until the drumhead is sufficiently tight, then tie the ends of these lacings together as in C. The drumhead should be tight enough so that it lies smooth and even across its entire surface, and reverberates when thumped with the fingers.

The next task is the stretching of the four thongs across the back as shown in D. These thongs are about three-eighths inch wide and twice the diameter of the drum in length. Slip them through the loops of the side lacing as illustrated, twist them, and tie. Do not pull these thongs too tight for fear of producing too much tension on the drumhead. With the four thongs all in place, cut a short string of rawhide and tie the four together where they cross at the center.

Be sure to wet the hide every few minutes during construction by rubbing water on it with the hand.

Occasionally one sees a drum of this type with tacks driven in the edges to furnish additional support for the drumhead, but their use should be avoided in favor of the Indian method of binding the rawhide to the wood through holes burnt in the sides, for the sake of a good drum and an authentic Indian job. A drum constructed as described above should not need additional support, but for safety's sake the additional side lacings may well be added—these are described on the following page and illustrated in Figure 13.

Single-headed drums are held by grasping the thongs where they cross at the back. When the drum has dried a more convenient hold can be made by stripping up cloth and wrapping it around the thongs where they cross each other, thus producing a round ball of the right size to fit the hand.

Hang the drum up to dry for twenty-four hours, following carefully the instructions on page 49.

Single-headed drums of this type call for one of the hard or semi-hard thumpers described in Chapter VII.

Another Method of Making a Single-Headed Drum.—There is another and perhaps more effective method of making a single-headed drum that is widely used among the Sioux,

Blackfeet, and other Plains tribes, as well as among the Indians of the Northwest Coast and Alaska. This method is illustrated in Figure 13. Holes should be burnt through the hoop at intervals of two inches all the way around it, as shown in A, Figure 13, this being done with a red-hot wire. The hide is cut to somewhat of a rectangular shape as shown in B, wide enough so that the sides will fold over the edge of the hoop and extend

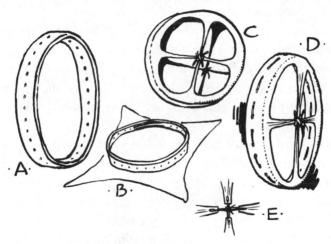

Fig. 13—*Another method of making a Single-headed Drum.*

over onto the back side about an inch, as indicated in C. Place the hide over the hoop and tack temporarily, stretching it just tight enough so that it is straight and smooth, without wrinkles, and reverberates when gently struck. Now pull the four corners across the back and tie them together at the center as shown in C, removing the tacks as you do so. Some of the hide on these four corner strips may then be cut away so as to give the back the appearance shown in C.

In case the hide is so small that the four points will not reach the center so as to be tied, they may be fastened together by the arrangement shown in E, Figure 13. Trim off the four ends so that they are equidistant from the center, cut a hole in the end of each and run rawhide thongs through these holes and tie together as shown.

Now from scraps of the rawhide we must cut a thong one-quarter inch wide, following the method described on page 45, and illustrated in C, Figure 7, long enough to go around the edge of the drumframe with a foot to spare. Next, run a pointed instrument through each of the holes that have been burnt in the frame, going through them from the under side and thus piercing the rawhide. Run the thong through these holes, following the method indicated in D, Figure 13. Stretch it tightly and tie the two ends together. This thong supplies additional support to the drumhead and makes a much more substantial drum.

One frequently sees a drum made in this way but without the lacing through the holes in the frame, the hide being merely tied in the center at the back. The drumhead on such drums is usually so loose as to make the instrument ineffective, and therefore the side lacing is strongly recommended.

If desired, a larger hand hold may be made where the rawhide is tied together in the middle of the back by wrapping this intersection with several strips of cloth until a knob is created of a convenient size to fit the hand.

This completes the drum and it is ready to dry. Follow the instructions given on page 49.

A Third Method of Making a Single-Headed Drum.—Still another method of making a hoop drum sometimes seen among the Blackfeet Indians is shown in Figure 14. This calls for a second and narrower hoop placed over the top of the main hoop at the drumhead edge. This narrower hoop should be about three-quarters of an inch wide and one-eighth of an inch thick. When it is in place holes should be burnt through the two hoops at intervals of every two inches and a long rawhide thong run

·A·   ·B·

through them and tied, as indicated in A, Figure 14. The hide is then placed over the frame and tied at the back as shown in B, or by either of the two methods described on the preceding pages for the making of single-headed drums.

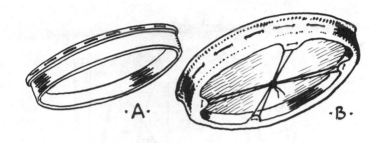

Fig. 14—*A Blackfoot Single-headed Drum.*

Now, with a hot wire, burn holes through the drumframe and hide just behind the ridge caused by the second hoop and run a long rawhide through these holes and tie tightly, as shown in B, Figure 14. The presence of the ridge caused by placing one hoop over the other provides additional tension on the drumhead when this thong is in place, and serves to produce a drum that will be affected less by weather changes.

THE PEGGED DRUM

The various tribes of the Sioux in long years past made a type of single-headed drum by inserting pegs through holes in the frame as shown in Figure 15. The pegs were of various styles and sizes, the better craftsmen making slender pins of hardwood such as those shown in the drawing. They are two and a half inches long, three-eighths inch wide at the top, and taper down to a sharp point.

To make such a drum, stretch the hide over the frame and tack it temporarily as in making other drums. With a small boring tool make a row of holes through the rawhide and frame midway between the edges of the hoop, spacing the holes two inches apart. Insert a peg into each of these holes as shown in the drawing. The pegs should be of such thickness that they

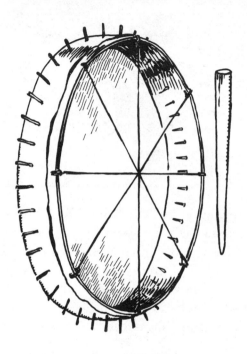

Fig. 15—*A Pegged Sioux Drum.*

can be inserted for a distance of one half their length. In the interest of a neat job, the holes should all be made the same size, and the pegs of uniform dimensions, so that the pins will all extend out the same distance. For this reason it is better to use a boring tool than to burn the holes through the wood with a hot wire.

Across the back side of this drum two thongs are stretched at right angles to each other to serve as a grip for the hand.

These thongs are tied through holes bored a half inch from the back edge of the frame.

The Tacked Single-Headed Drums

Single-headed drums can be quickly constructed by tacking the hide to the sides of the frame. Tacks make a good drum but scarcely an authentic one of the ancient Indian pattern. Brass-headed tacks add a decorative touch.

SQUARE HAND-DRUMS

Square drums have been used by the Indians of the Northwest Coast these many years, how long we know not—probably always—and in recent times have become somewhat prevalent among the Plains Indians because of the ever-present packingbox. Unknown among the Chippewas of the woods who have access to an abundance of the best wood for circular hoops in white cedar, the Sioux, Blackfeet and other Plains peoples have resorted to them occasionally of late owing to their difficulty in getting good wood for hoops, to the ease of obtaining suitable lumber for square frames, and to the fact that a square frame can be made in a fraction of the time required to make a good hoop frame.

A square frame makes every bit as good a drum as a round one, and might enjoy a popularity comparable to it were it not for the fact that they seem to smack of modern times even though occasional tribes have long used them. No amount of Indian decoration can cover up the fact that there is a packing-box within, and to one who likes old Indian ways, this truth shouts at him every time he looks at it.

An easy solution to drumframe materials is found in the square drum and to those who are interested only in securing a serviceable drum and care nothing about atmosphere, it is probably almost as good as any in case a hoop frame cannot be constructed. A makeshift hoop frame from a cheese-box as described later in this chapter is to be preferred to a square frame in that it follows the traditional pattern of most Indian tribes. Since the square drum has long been used by the Indians of the Northwest Coast, and is employed by some other tribes today, it will be described in this section as an authentic Indian drum before taking up the imitations of Indian drumframes from modern materials that can be easily picked up.

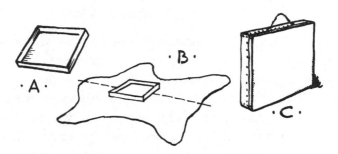

Fig. 16—*Making a Square Hand-drum.*

From packing-box lumber secure boards one-quarter inch thick. Of course if you can secure white-cedar boards and cut them to size, so much the better, for no wood will make so good a drum. The width of the boards should be two inches, the length depending on the size of the drum desired, twelve to fifteen inches being recommended as desirable for small square drums. Nail together these pieces into a square frame as in A, Figure 16, and round off the edges and corners slightly with a knife so that they will not cut the hide.

Lay the hide on the floor, hair side down, flesh side up, and place the frame on it as shown in B, Figure 16. Double the hide at the neck end up and tack it near the top edge with a row of carpet tacks. Now take hold of the hide at the tail end, stretch it over the top side of the frame, fold it down over the edge and tack it along the middle of the frame with brass-headed tacks, as shown in C, Figure 16; it will be noted that the first row of carpet tacks is covered up by this second fold of hide, thus showing only the brass-headed tacks. Complete the tacking of the other two sides of the frame in the same way. Trim off the excess hide neatly and tack the loose edges of the hide at the corners with additional tacks. Tack on a thong of hide for a handle as shown and the drum is completed. The detailed description of making the Chippewa war-drums (pages 44 to 49) should be read for details of drumcraft. The hide should be stretched, before being tacked, just tight enough so that it lies flat and smooth, and reverberates when the finger is snapped against it. Remember to keep the hide wet throughout the process of making the drum.

Dry the drum as described on page 49.

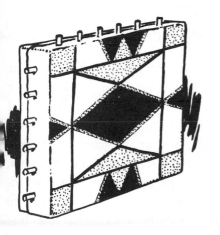

Fig. 17—*A Pegged Square Drum from the Sioux.*

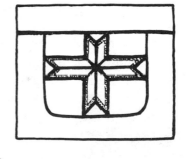

Fig. 18—*A Sioux square-drum design.*

Figure 17 shows an ancient square drum from the Sioux and Figure 18 shows the design on another old Sioux drum.

Occasionally drums are made rectangular in shape instead

of square. Such styles are often seen among the Karok Indians of Northern California, a common size being fourteen by eighteen by five inches.

Huge square drums measuring up to four feet may be constructed in just the same way as the small ones. The frame for these over-size drums should be six to eight inches wide.

Laced Square Drums.—Square drums are often made by lacing the drumheads together following the methods for making the hoop-drums described earlier in this chapter.

Pegged Square Drums.—The Dakotas frequently pegged the hide to the frame in making square drums, using the method already described for round drums under the heading, "The Pegged Drum." Figure 17 shows such a drum, the pegs being one-quarter inch in diameter and extending out from the frame a half inch.

MEDICINE HAND-DRUMS

Medicine—spirit power—is contained in many types of drums according to the beliefs of various Indian tribes. Whatever the type of drum, whether it be hand-drum, big dance-drum, or two-headed log-drum, there are sure to be certain styles of it that are supposed to possess unusual potency, and therefore labelled as *medicine drums* and reserved as sacred for those occasions when the medicine in question is needed. For example, the big dance-drums described in Chapter V, painted with certain designs, and ornamented in certain ways, are thought to possess unusual spirit power and are never used except in certain religious dances. Similarly certain types of water-drums are considered

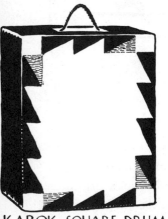

KAROK SQUARE DRUM

as potent agencies. So, too, with the hand-drums in this chapter.

The war-drums or chief's drums of the Chippewas and neighboring woodland tribes, constructed by lacing rawhide over a cedar hoop as described earlier in this chapter, are merely drums for providing rhythm for war-dances and similar activities—they possess no unusual potency. However, when certain rattle devices are added the drum becomes a medicine drum of power, which, minus the rattles, it would not have. These rattle devices give a sort of snare-drum effect when the drum is struck and many prefer to add them in making drums for use today. The rattles are of two types—*strung rattles* and *loose rattles,* each having a peculiar influence of their own. The strung type consists of stick-rattles, bead-rattles and plain string-rattles. Drums with these strung rattles are sometimes called "medicine war-drums"; however, if they possess stick-rattles of the type shown in Figure 19, they frequently go by the name of "moccasin-game drums" among the Chippewas, owing to the fact that drums of this type are used while playing the moccasin game.

As contrasted to the medicine war-drums or moccasin-game drums with strung rattles, those with loose rattles in the form of pebbles inside are true medicine drums, used by medicine men in treating the sick. These are usually very small in size, commonly around eight inches in diameter and are used both as a shaking rattle and as a drum.

The average drum purchased from the Indians will not possess any of these types of medicine rattles, the typical old Indian who is true to his faith being reluctant to sell such a drum to a white man.

Each of these types of medicine hand-drums will be considered in turn.

Strung Medicine Rattles

Strung rattles consist of stick-rattles, bead-rattles, and

string-rattles, installed either inside or outside the drum:

Stick-Rattles Strung Inside the Drum.—Stick-rattles, the type used in the medicine war-drum and moccasin-game drum, add much interest to any hand-drum in that the many little sticks within strike against the drumhead each time the drum is struck and produce a soft tapping sound on the order of that obtained from a snare drum. We thus have the full strong sound from the drumstick and between beats, the constant tapping of the rattle sticks against the reverberating drumhead. People who are unfamiliar with the construction of Indian tomtoms wonder, on listening to the drum, how the snare effect—the constant rattling or tapping—is achieved. These rattles can be added while making any two-headed hand-drum built over a hoop frame.

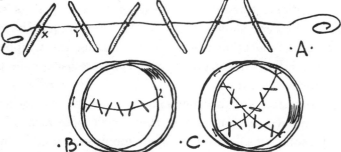

Fig. 19—*Medicine Stick-rattles inside the drum.*

There are two kinds of stick-rattles, the simplest form being shown in A, Figure 19. Six little sticks two inches long are tied to a string as shown in A, and the string tied to the inside of the drumframe as in B. Kitchen matches are just the right size and one can do no better than to cut off the heads of a half dozen matches and use the sticks by tying them to the string at the middle as shown in A, Figure 19. It will be noted that the adjacent sticks in A slant in different directions, this being caused by the pressure of the knot, the direction depending on which side of the stick the knot is tied—for example, the knot at X is visible on the front side of the stick, whereas on the next stick, Y, it is on the back side and not visible.

With the six sticks tied to the string as illustrated, install the string in the drumframe as illustrated in B. Note that it extends directly across the center of the hoop and that it is loose enough so that it sags about one inch at the center. The string should be against one of the drumheads—burn a hole a half inch or less from the edge of the frame, run the end of the string through it and tie around the edge of the frame.

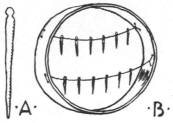

Fig. 20—*Another type of Stick-rattle for Medicine Drums.*

Now prepare a second string and attach it in the same way at right angles to the first as shown in C. This second string should be placed against the opposite drumhead so that there will be sticks tapping against both drumheads when the drum is struck.

In a single-headed drum the strings of rattles are placed inside the drum, both against the one drumhead.

Stick-rattles of the second type are larger and of different shape. From any kind of hardwood whittle out a dozen pins of the shape shown in A, Figure 20. These are about four and one-half inches long and one-quarter inch thick at the large end, tapering down to a fine point. The groove near the top end is for the string. Tie six of these to each string and attach to the drumframe as shown in B—note that one is suspended above the other, and that each sags about one inch at the center.

Place one string against one drumhead and the other against the other, tying them to the frame through holes, as described in the preceding paragraphs.

These rattles, being larger and heavier, produce a different sound effect than the other type—they strike less often and give less of a snare effect, but make a louder sound.

Fig. 21—*Medicine rattles strung outside the drum.*

Stick-Rattles Strung Outside the Drum.—Figure 21 shows a finished drum with a string of stick-rattles attached *outside* the drumhead. These are rare as compared to the inside type but are occasionally seen among the Chippewas and other tribes of similar culture. While small sticks, such as those in A, Figure 19, may be used, it is better to make these outside rattles from quills of large feathers for the reason that the quills may be slipped to one side when not in use. Strip the webb off of turkey or other large feathers, leaving only the quill, and cut these into sections about two and a half inches long. Using a darning needle threaded to strong, smooth-finished string, force the needle through the quills and pull the string through, leaving the quills suspended on the string but not tied—they can thus be shoved along the string but the friction is sufficient to keep them from moving of their own accord.

When the rattle effect is desired spread the quills as in Figure 21, but when the drum is not in use or the rattle effect is not wanted, shove them to one side as illustrated.

Bead-Rattles.—Among the Woodland Indians and occasional Plains tribes in recent years, beads have sometimes been used instead of sticks on strung rattles. Six or eight small beads of the type used in beading moccasins or clothing are strung on the cord, spaced an inch or two apart. The strings are installed either outside or inside the drum in exactly the same way as are the stick-rattles, except that they are stretched very tightly. Although the bead-rattles produce a typical snare-drum sound, they are less effective than the stick-rattles.

String-Rattles.—Occasionally one sees an old Indian drum from the Northwoods with nothing more than a plain string of buckskin or cord stretched tightly across the drumhead. This string produces a soft snare sound when the drum is struck. The Slav Indians, hunters of the Northwest Canadian woods, used such an arrangement.

Loose Rattles

Drums containing the strung rattles described above, particularly the stick-rattles, carry the names of medicine war-drums and moccasin-game drums among the Chippewas while those with pebble rattles are true medicine drums. The difference in the medicine powers that these two types are supposed to possess, I do not know, and probably never will, for the old-type Indian keeps his more sacred beliefs to himself when around white men, and while he may have many answers to one's questions, the real meaning usually is carefully concealed. And the young and talkative, educated Indian, more often than not, is not reliable anyway.

One thing is certain, however—the medicine drums with pebble rattles are the ones used by the medicine men in treating the sick among the Chippewa, Winnebago, Menominee, Sauk-Fox, Slav, and similar woodland tribes. While these drums are of several sizes, they run smaller than war-drums, a 15-inch diameter being considered an unusually large one.

The drum is made just like an ordinary two-headed war-drum or chief's drum as described earlier in this chapter, except that a good-sized handful of very small pebbles is placed inside it before the lacing is completed.

Figure 22 shows an old medicine drum from the Wisconsin Chippewas, once the property of Aniwabi (Eniwûbe), a medicine man. It is large for a medicine drum — fifteen inches in

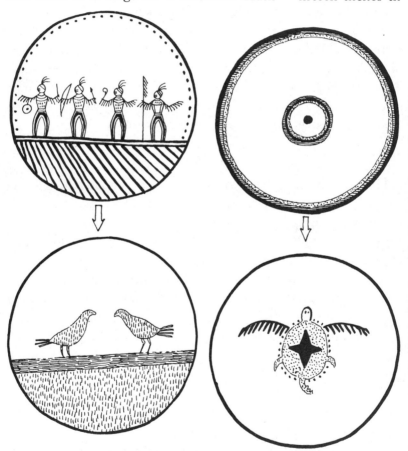

Fig. 22—*Designs from a Chippewa Medicine Hand-drum—this drum has designs on both sides of the two heads.*

diameter. Note the decorations painted on the hide, particularly the fact that there are designs on the *inside* of the drumheads also.

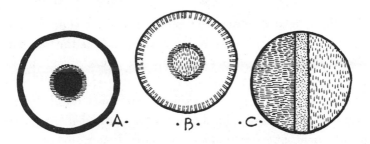

Fig. 23—*Three Chippewa Medicine Drums, eight inches in diameter.*

More typically these medicine drums are very small, from two to eight inches in diameter, and from a half to three-quarters of an inch in thickness—Figure 23 shows three of these. The reason for the small size is that they are used as rattles more often than as drums; that is, they are shaken with the hand, producing the drumming sound by throwing the pebbles against the drumhead. The medicine man, sitting or kneeling beside the stricken one, manipulates the medicine drum over him with his hand.

To make one of these eight-inch medicine drums, cut a strip of white cedar thirty inches long and three-quarters inch wide, soak it well and bend it into a hoop seven or eight inches in diameter, following the detailed instructions previously outlined. Of the materials obtainable in the city, a piece of a cheese-box will serve admirably (see page 72). Cover both sides of the frame with rawhide, put a handful of small pebbles inside and lace as described on page 46.

The decorations for medicine drums are described and illustrated later in this chapter under the heading "Indian Hand-Drum Designs."

A few of these little medicine drums are excellent additions to a rhythm band.

HAND-DRUMS FROM ANY OLD THING

For those who do not have access to white cedar nor have the patience and skill to split a board from a cedar log, whittle it down, and bend it into a hoop for the drumframe, the lowly *cheese-box* obtainable from any grocery store will provide material from which a serviceable frame for a hand-drum can be quickly and easily made. Similarly, hand-drums can be made from *mixing-bowls, tin-cans,* and *flower saucers.*

Cheese-Box Drums

When drum-making is used as a craft for children it is obvious that whittling and bending the hoop from cedar is impractical for all except the most mature, skilled, and thoroughly interested children. For the others the cheese-box is an easy solution for the making of drums that when finished will have all the appearances of authentic Indian war-drums. The making of the frame is always the difficult part of drum construction, but happily, cheese-boxes are already bent into a circular shape.

The wood in a cheese-box is so thin that it will warp and bend out of shape under the pressure of the rawhide as it tightens, and for this reason the hoop must be made of two layers of cheese-box wood, one placed outside the other. Take the cheese-box apart, using a pair of pliers to withdraw the nails and being as careful as possible not to split it. With a knife and saw cut off from the circular box two hoops, each two inches or two and a quarter inches wide, both exactly the same width and length.

There are two methods that may be used in lacing these two hoops together to create one hoop with sufficient strength. One

is illustrated in Figure 24: Place one hoop inside the other and
with a hot wire burn the two holes shown at X in A, Figure 24.
Run a thong of wet rawhide through these holes and tie tightly
as shown. Then burn the two holes at Y in A and tie as shown.
Continue burning holes every two inches all around the hoop,
tying with rawhide as you go, until the hoop appears as in B.
Overlap the two ends and lace together as indicated at Z in B.
This method produces a substantial frame but has a ridge at Z
that will show through the rawhide when the drum is completed. This may be relieved by thinning the ridge down with
a knife, but to avoid it completely the other method of lacing
the hoops together must be used.

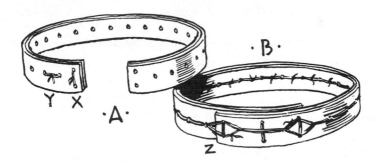

Fig. 24 –*Making a hoop from cheese-box wood.*

The second method of preparing the cheese-box hoops is
shown in Figure 25. Bring the ends of one hoop together, burn
the six holes shown in A and lace as illustrated, thus holding
the ends together without forming a ridge. Now place the
second hoop outside this one in such a way that its ends are
at the opposite side from the laced ends of the first hoop, as
indicated in B. Burn holes in the ends of the second hoop in the
same way as in the first, and lace together as in B. The ends
of the second or outer hoop will not quite meet but that makes
no difference. Then burn holes through both layers every two

inches all around the hoop as shown in B, and run a long thong of wet rawhide through them and tie, following the plan clearly shown in B. When the rawhide dries the two hoops will be firmly bound into one.

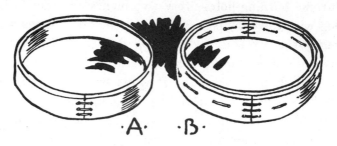

Fig. 25—*Another method of making a cheese-box hoop frame.*

Having constructed the drumframe by one of these methods, complete the drum by covering it with rawhide and lacing the edges together just as described for the authentic Chippewa war-drum on page 46. If rawhide is not available one of the substitutes such as paper, cloth or rubber may be used—drums constructed of these are described on page 29.

The cheese-box frame will produce a good drum, not comparable of course to one made from a solid cedar hoop, but a very serviceable one nevertheless. Occasionally the cheese-box frame will warp even when made double, but this is not apt to happen unless the drum is a very large one. Sometimes an unpleasant rattle develops in a drum with a cheese-box frame that can be distinctly heard as the drum reverberates, due probably to the fact that the two hoops were not laced together firmly enough.

Mixing-Bowl Drums

The kitchen mixing-bowl or chopping-bowl furnishes a ready-made drumframe from which a tomtom can be fashioned in a half an hour. The drumhead can either be tacked down as shown in B, Figure 26, or laced as shown in C. Obviously no effort is being made to produce an authentic Indian drum in the use of a mixing-bowl and consequently the tacking is entirely acceptable, and is to be recommended since it will produce a tighter, neater, and more serviceable drum. Brass-headed tacks placed an inch apart around the top edge of the mixing-bowl, as shown in B, gives the drum an attractive appearance. If the drum is to be laced as in C, the same general method is followed as described for the single-headed Indian drums on page 56.

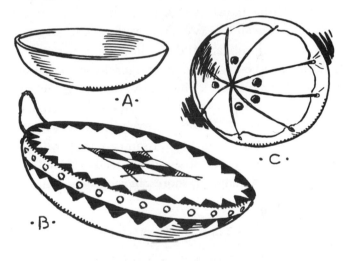

Fig. 26—*A mixing-bowl drum.*

Whichever of these two methods is to be used—the tacking or the lacing—the detailed descriptions of the two-headed Chippewa war-drum and the single-headed hand-drum presented earlier in this chapter, should be carefully read before undertaking the task. Whatever the nature of the frame the same general techniques apply and, therefore, there is no need to repeat the detailed process of construction and drying.

If rawhide is not available for the drumhead, use one of the substitutes described on page 29.

A handle may be made for the chopping-bowl drum by tacking the ends of an eight-inch strip of rawhide to the bowl near the top edge, but the preferred method of holding this type of drum is to bore three to five holes near the center of the bottom as shown in C, Figure 26, through which the fingers may be inserted.

One can scarcely anticipate that the mixing-bowl drum will produce the same rich, full, reverberating tone that is obtained from a war-drum made over a cedar hoop. The wood in the bowl is so thick and heavy that it does not respond to the beating of the drumhead, and the bottom is covered so solidly with wood that, even with the finger holes bored in it, the sound does not have much chance to escape. The result is often a sharp, dead, thumping sound as compared to that produced by the lighter drums. However, experimentation will usually find one or two spots on the drumhead that will produce a pleasing tone. The center of the drumhead is usually dead and flat, while near the edges a more characteristic tomtom sound is emitted.

Tin-Can War-Drums

A hoop cut from a tin can will provide an excellent frame for a small tomtom of the war-drum type. The best source for such a tin hoop is one of the round tin candy boxes so popular at Christmas time. These are usually about eight to ten inches wide and two inches deep, and consequently produce a tin hoop of just the right proportions for a small war-drum when the lid has been removed and the bottom cut out with a can-opener.

If one of these cannot be found, a two-inch hoop may be cut

from the top of a large cookie can, a Number 10 vegetable can, or any can seven inches or more in diameter.

Having secured the tin hoop, proceed to cover it with the rawhide (or one of the substitutes described on page 29) and

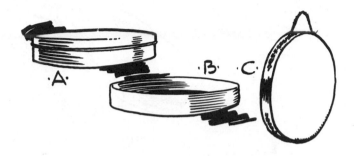

Fig. 27—*A hand-drum from a tin candy-box.*

to lace the edges just as described for making the authentic Chippewa war-drum on page 44. Since a tin-can drum is a makeshift arrangement most people do not take the same pains in making than would be the case if they were using better materials, and so the results are often inferior, but if the work is carefully done and one follows all of the instructions given for the Chippewa war-drum, a very satisfactory little drum should result. True, the somewhat metallic sound which these drums invariably have, publishes the fact that there is tin within even though it cannot be seen, but if well made, the tone, even though slightly tinny, is nevertheless pleasant.

Here is an excellent source of drum materials for children they take to tin drums with zest and enthusiasm always.

Flower-Saucer Drum

A tiny hand-drum can be made merely by stretching a piece of rawhide over the top of the saucer to a flowerpot and fastening it by wrapping a long string of rawhide around the edge and tying it, as shown in Figure 28. The use of these saucers provides an interesting novelty for the drum-making activities of children's music classes and clubs.

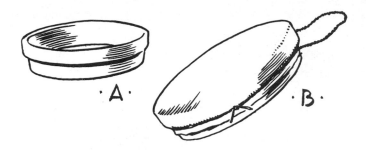

Fig. 28—*A flower-saucer drum.*

DRUM DECORATIONS

No drum of the Indian pattern should be considered complete until it has been duly decorated—indeed, the decorating process should be considered a part of the actual making of the drum and if at all possible should be consummated at the same time that the drum is constructed and before the hide has dried. The Indian always added a bit of color in the way of decorative and usually symbolic designs—minus these, the drum somehow seems un-Indian and otherwise definitely fails in achieving its full attractiveness.

Drum decoration consists first and primarily of designs painted on the drumhead, and secondly, of ornamentation applied to the drumframe.

Painting the Drumheads

In the old days the Indians used natural dyes and colorings made by themselves in applying designs to their drumheads, but needless to say the making of these colorings is not to be recommended as practical for general use today; neither are they used any longer by the Indians themselves except in rare cases, practically all tribes now relying upon commercial colorings.

A *watercolor* of some type is necessary for drumheads, no other type of paint being usable. *Paint powder, colored chalk, caked watercolors* and *show-card paint* are all acceptable, but among present-day Indians the paint powder receives the choice nine times out of ten and is strongly recommended in that it gives a certain primitiveness and elemental quality to the drum that seems to be so often lost if more refined paints are applied. Colored paint powders or pigments in a variety of colors may be obtained from any paint store or large hardware store. When enough water has been mixed with this powder to produce a thin paste, we have the ideal coloring for rawhide drumheads. A refined type of paint powder may be obtained in cans from art stores, but for our purpose it has few advantages over the inexpensive powder used and sold at ordinary paint stores.

Three or four strong, full colors are all that is needed—a medium shade of *blue*, a medium *yellow*, a vivid *red*, and a *green*.

Since much better results will be obtained if the drumhead is painted immediately after the drum is finished and before the hide has dried, we shall consider the painting of wet rawhide first and then take up the methods that must be used after the drum has dried. Provide a saucer or tin-can cover for each color of paint powder and put about a tablespoonful of each colored powder into its saucer. Add just enough water to each to make a thin paste. So mixed and applied to the wet rawhide, the paint will remain permanently fixed after the drum is dry, but if a little of it falls off the general effect is enhanced if anything, taking on a characteristic, handmade, primitive atmosphere. With a pencil sketch the design on the drumhead, and apply the paint by the Indian's method of using the fingers and a pointed stick. While small paint brushes may be used they are not at all necessary, three or four sharpened match-sticks being ideal for the fine lines and the finger for the solid spots. By selecting an authentic design as described later in this chapter, using a paint powder of this type and applying it by these methods, an Indian tomtom will be produced that will ring true in every respect.

Another method of applying the design to a wet drumhead is to use ordinary colored crayon—merely mark the chalk on the wet drumhead, giving it the desired design and coloring. When the drum has dried the coloring will be fixed and permanent. Colored chalk will not produce as bold and strong a design as will the paint powder and is recommended only when ther colorings are not available.

Liquid show-card paint is excellent and comes already mixed and ready for use in delightful shades, but is more expensive than the paint powder. Neither liquid show-card paint nor caked water-colors will come off when applied to wet rawhide. In using these types of paint, only the bold, strong colors should be selected, these being preferable always in Indian decorating to mixed colors and soft, delicate tones.

In painting a *dry drum* a little glue must be added to the paint in order to make it stick. Colored chalk is not usable at all on a dry drumhead and caked water-colored paints are not recommended. Paint powder is the best: mix enough water with it to make a thin paste as described above and add a few drops of liquid glue and mix thoroughly. With the glue added there is no danger of the paint scaling off as the drum is beaten.

Occasionally one sees a present-day Indian-made drum that has been decorated with ordinary wax crayon rubbed on the dry hide, but while this may produce a permanent and enduring decoration it is not an attractive one and does not seem in harmony with the spirit of a primitive drum.

Drumframe Decorations

Fig. 29—*A Chippewa Medicine War-Drum.*

A common practice among the Chippewa Indians is to cover the edge of the war-drum with a strip of fur glued and tacked to it. Such a drum is shown in Figure 29. While this gives a rich and finished appearance to the drum it is not at all necessary, and even among the Chippewas was used only on their better drums. A neatly-made drum with a good design painted on the rawhide is attractive enough without the addition of a covering for the edge of the frame. Occasionally one sees a modern Indian drum with a strip of felt glued around the frame thus covering up the laced rawhide edge but the felt is less attractive than the rawhide itself and gives a modern touch to it that is detrimental. If fur cannot be obtained the edge of the drum is better left uncovered.

Beaver fur is the choice above all others of the Chippewa

Indian for decorating drums, hats, headdresses, clothing—in fact, for every purpose where fur is added for ornamental reasons. To the Chippewa, no fur can equal in beauty that of the beaver. Among my fur-covered drums, however, I have one covered with wolf and another with bear.

The fur used for covering the edges of Indian drums is usually rawhide rather than tanned, although tanned fur would be better for obvious reasons. Cut the fur into strips the exact width of the drumframe and glue them to the edge of the drum, reenforcing the glue occasionally with small tacks.

If you are fortunate enough to secure raw beaver fur with which to cover the drum, a group of fur tassels should be added on each side as shown in Figure 29. To make these tassels cut up strips of the raw beaver hide a half an inch wide and twelve inches long. Soak these in water for a half an hour, then twist them until they take on the appearance of the tassel. Tie a string to each end and suspend the tassel in the air until dried, stretching the string tightly. When dry it will keep its tassel or tail-like shape permanently. Eight or ten of these tassels ill be needed, four or five to be tied into a cluster and then tacked to the side of the drumframe slightly above its middle as shown in Figure 29.

A drum covered with untanned fur must be carefully guarded from moths, for these pests will single it out above all other delicacies the house may offer.

Among the Sioux a common method of decorating the drumframe is to attach four or six eagle feathers to the edge as shown in the illustration of the Sioux drum in Figure 30. Small feathers no longer than eight inches in length should be selected. These can be attached while the drum is being made by cutting small slits in the wet rawhide and running a thong of buckskin or a string through them, which in turn is attached to the end of the quill. If the feathers are to be attached after the drum has dried, small tacks should be driven into the frame to which string is tied.

Occasionally steer's horns are attached to the drumframe as is the case on the Cheyenne drum seen in Figure 31.

Fig. 30—*A single-headed Sioux drum with eagle feathers.*

One frequently sees an Indian-made hand-drum with the edges of the frame painted in a solid color to correspond with the coloring on the drumhead. Seldom is a design painted on the frame, the use of solid colors being the usual practice. The drums from British Columbia shown in Figure 51 have frames painted in this way.

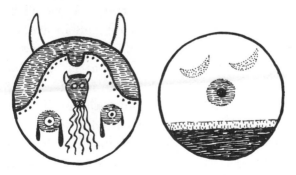

Fig. 31—*Two Cheyenne drum designs.*

Indian Hand-Drum Designs

All who are familiar with Indian art will agree that there is a peculiar element in Indian decorative and symbolic design that is extremely difficult for other peoples to achieve completely unless the Indian design is accurately copied. The designs of the various tribes differ somewhat in appearance, and particularly in symbolic meaning, but there is a sameness in the general type of designs among the tribes of the various culture areas—for example, all of the Southwest tribes produce designs that give much the same impression; likewise the geometric patterns of the various tribes of Plains Indians are much alike, and differ from the floral designs so common among the woods-dwelling Indians; all of these types differ from the totem effect characteristic of the Northwest tribes. Whatever the source of the design, however, a true Indian atmosphere is much better achieved by copying than by improvising. For this reason a generous supply of authentic hand-drum designs is presented in these pages.

It is true that there is a loss in creativity in any craft that requires copying rather than originality. There is no reason why a policy of creating symbolic and decorative designs of Indian type cannot be adopted, but hope for success in this rests in long familiarity with true Indian patterns. It would be a mistake to apply to an authentically-made Indian drum a design that is so far removed from the typical Indian style in drum decoration that any informed person could tell at a glance that it does not belong there—so decorated, the drum just does not hang together. So, if you would have a drum with true Indian atmosphere, study the patterns here presented, and either copy or adhere strictly to the general style. Remember that Indian design is seldom if ever realistic, but always either symbolic or at least merely suggestive, leaving much to the imagination.

There is often a certain irregularity to Indian drum decoration, a sort of unfinished quality, which causes the observer to label the work as "crude." A little study, however, convinces one that these irregularities and the primitive simplicity greatly enhance the imaginative appeal and atmosphere. The chief stumbling block in executing this type of decoration is the desire to use a preciseness, a delicacy, and a "neatness" that smacks immediately of the machine-made world, and lacks the boldness, the freedom, and the unrestraint of the drum designs from the open country. True, many Indian drum designs contain geometric figures, such as stars for example, that are intricate, precise, and perfectly balanced, but there is nevertheless a primitive, woodsy irregularity to the general effect, owing to the type of painting.

All designs shown in these pages are copied from old drums or at least from drums made by old Indians. They are all true to the culture of the tribe in question.

Many old Indian drums with double heads have a design on the *inside* of the drumhead in addition to the one on the outside, invisible to the eye, of course, but the Indian who made it knows it is there and it gives the drum an added symbolic meaning to him. The medicine drum illustrated in Figure 22 has such inside designs. We see much the same idea in designs painted on the inside of the soles of moccasins made by the Dakotas. Single-headed Alaskan drums and some from the Northwest Coast are decorated on the *inside only*.

Designs from Woodland Tribes.—Let us consider first the details of the Chippewa decoration on their two-headed drums. Typically these Chippewa hand-drums have one highly ornamented drumhead while the other head contains only a colored spot in the center, but whatever this spot may lack in decorative quality it makes up in symbolic importance to the Indian. What meaning it has I know not, but tradition demands that it be there in some form or other, and the tradition is definitely backed up by religious significance. Whatever else you wish to put on the drum, see to it that there is a round spot in the center on one drumhead.

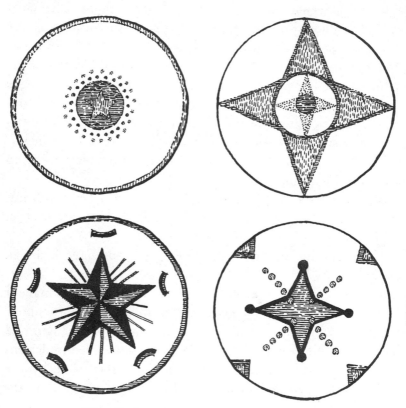

Fig. 32—*Star designs from Chippewa drums.*

The Chippewa drum designs, with many individual variations, fall for the most part under the following types: (1) *star designs*, (2) *designs symbolizing the world or universe*, (3) *thunderbirds*, (4) *turtles*, (5) *men and living quarters.*

Figures 32 and 33 show typical Chippewa *star designs*, the star figure being very common on the drums of this tribe. Most of these are from drums coming originally from the Northern Wisconsin Chippewas. Another example is seen in the fine Chippewa medicine war-drum with stick-rattles, twenty-four inches in diameter, both sides of which are shown in Figure 29;

Fig. 33—*Star designs from Chippewa drums.*

one side has a round red spot three inches in diameter in the center, with no other decoration on that side save a half-inch stripe of yellow around the circumference; both the spot and the stripe would be put on with the finger rather than brushes, with little effort to make it decorative, this spot side being for *medicine.* The opposite side has a complicated four-pointed

Fig. 34—*Chippewa drum designs representing the universe.*

star in red and blue. The edge of the frame is covered with beaver fur with side tassels of beaver added (see page 81).

The designs shown in Figures 34 and 35, also from original Wisconsin Chippewa drums, are of the type that represent the *world* or the *universe*, each having a symbolic meaning of its own. An interesting example of these is A, Figure 35: The edge with the triangles represents the ocean; the two lines at right angles to each other across the center, the world; the drapery effect symbolizes storm clouds; the two small spots with zigzag lines running down represent lightning, and the two large spots

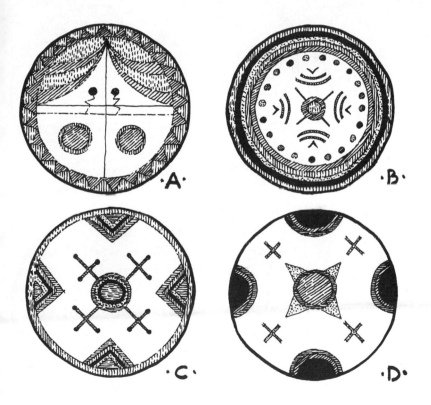

Fig. 35—*Chippewa drum designs representing the universe.*

below, thunder. The whole constitutes a thunderstorm symbol. The coloring is in blue and red, blue predominating.

Thunderbirds of the Chippewa type are shown on the drums in Figure 36. The *turtle* which appears so often on Chippewa drums is shown in Figure 37, and in more symbolic form in Figure 22. *Dancing and fighting men* are seen on one of the drumheads in Figure 22.

Fig. 36—*Chippewa thunderbird designs.*

The old medicine drum with pebble-rattles shown in Figure 22 is one of the most interestingly and attractively decorated

tomtoms within my experience. During the process of moving one of its heads was accidently split, and to my surprise there were decorations on *both* sides of its two heads, those on the inside being completely hidden from view, but their presence was known to the old Indian who used it. And curiously enough, the designs on the inside were in vivid, bright colors while those on the outside were somber by comparison,

Fig. 37—*Chippewa turtle design.*

dark green lines with faint outlines of red. This drum was once owned and used by Aniwabi (Eniwûbe), one-time medicine man of the Chippewas in Northern Wisconsin and Eastern Minnesota.

Looking at the designs of this drum in Figure 22, we find the inevitable spot on one side, a tiny one three-quarters of an inch in diameter, in green, with a green circle around it, and a double circle around the outer edge, one green and the other dark red. On the reverse side of this head and invisible is the interesting turtle pattern (see arrow) executed in bright blue and yellow. On the outside of the other head we find the four dancers standing on the surface of the world with a row of dots around the top edge representing stars in the sky; the dancers are holding war weapons, one a war-drum, the next an arrow, the third a war-club and the last a spear, all with feathers on their arms suggesting an eagle or other bird dance, all these designs being in dark green with thin outlines and touchings of red. On the reverse side of this hide the invisible design consists of the two birds in blue as pictured, standing on a yellow strip beneath which is a solid blue mass.

The little medicine drums shown in A and B, Figure 23, each eight inches in diameter, have spots on each side, that shown in B having in addition a row of one-inch lines around the edge. A more typical Chippewa design for a small medicine drum, however, is that shown in C—a yellow strip one-half inch wide across the center, with solid blue on one side of it, and solid red on the other—this is the design used on the big dream-dance drum described in Chapter IV, and it has unusual significance to the Chippewas.

Figures 38 are selected from drums of the Northern Minnesota Chippewa which differ slightly in type of decoration from those of the Wisconsin area, these showing for the most part dome-shaped bark wigwams, pointed bark wigwams, and dancing or fighting figures.

Occasionally one sees a Chippewa war-drum with an eagle feather attached to the center of the spot that is sure to appear on one side. The feather must be attached while the hide is still

Fig. 38—*Minnesota Chippewa drum designs.*

wet in the process of making the drum. Such a drum is shown in Figure 39.

Most of the Chippewa designs referred to in the preceding paragraphs are quite typical of the Woodland Indians in general, particularly the Winnebago, Menominee, and Sauk-Fox tribes.

The drum showing the hand in Figure 40 is from the *Slav*

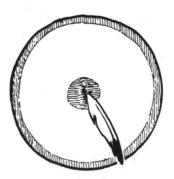

Fig. 39—*Chippewa drum with an eagle feather.*

Indians, hunters of the northwest Canadian woods. This hand design appears frequently on drums of the woods-dwelling and Plains Indians. The solid area is blue and the hand dark brown.

Fig. 40—*A Slav drum design.*

Plains Indian Drum Designs.—Two striking Arapaho designs are shown in Figures 41 and 42. That in Figure 41 is blue, including the sides, with red waves across the drum surface. The center circle is blue with a red line around it. In Figure 42 the

Fig. 41—*An Arapaho drum design.* Fig. 42—*An Arapaho drum design.*

background color is yellow, the pipe bowl red, and the dark areas deep green.

Two *Cheyenne* drum designs are illustrated in Figure 31. It will be noted that one of these has two short steer's horns attached to the frame.

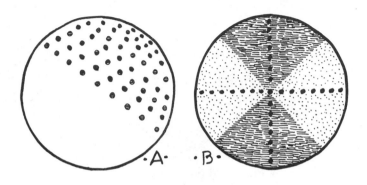

Fig. 43—*Blackfoot Indian drum designs.*

Typical *Blackfeet* drum designs are shown in Figures 43 and 44. That in A, Figure 43 contains nothing but rows of red and blue spots over one-half of the surface. In B, Figure 43, the solid areas are red and yellow, and the spots a deep brown. The simple design in Figure 44 has one half of the drumhead

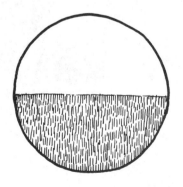

Fig. 44—*Blackfoot drum design.*

Fig. 45—*A Sioux drum.*

colored red, the other half remaining natural.

An interesting *Sioux* design is shown in Figure 45: the ground area at the bottom is blue and the sky red, the trees are green and the stars or spots in the sky are blue. Another typical *Dakota* design is the simple arrangement shown in

Fig. 46—*A simple Sioux design.*

Figure 46—one-half is red and the other blue. Typical Sioux square-drum designs are shown in Figures 17 and 18; the coloring is red and blue. The Sioux were much given to attaching eagle feathers to the drumframe as in Figure 30; the design on this drumhead shows a buffalo in red.

Frequently one sees drums among the Plains Indians deco-

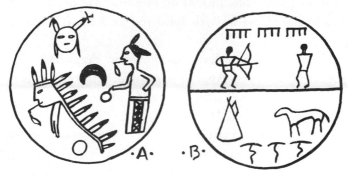

Fig. 47—*Story designs on Plains Indian drums.*

rated with historical sketches, that is, drawings that tell a story of past exploits, resembling the figures on the old buffalo hides used to record the painter's life history. Such drums are shown in Figure 47; A is a *Ute* drum but the source of B is unknown.

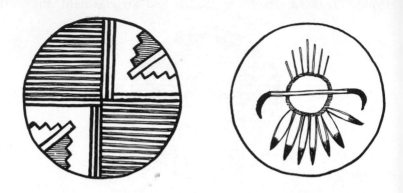

Fig. 48—*Pueblo hand-drum design.*   Fig. 49—*A Hopi hand-drum.*

These figures are in outline only and are usually drawn with red and blue.

Southwest Hand-Drum Designs.—Typical of the Rio Grande is the Pueblo design shown on the hand-drum in Figure 48. The solid triangular areas are red, and the heavy lines across the center green. The mountain symbols are outlined in green, the right half filled in with solid red and the left half remaining natural.

A Hopi hand-drum design is shown in Figure 49.

Figure 50 shows an Apache hand-drum pattern. It is red with blue circle and center spot. The edge of the drumframe is covered with a wide beaded band.

Northwest Coast Drum Designs.—Three hand-drums covered with caribou skin from the Gitskan Indians of British Columbia are shown in Figure 51. In A and B the center area is natural and the border in maroon. In C the solid dark areas are black, the center spot natural and the twelve round spots blue; the outer line around the edge is light blue, the next line natural, and the inner line red with cross-lines of blue. These

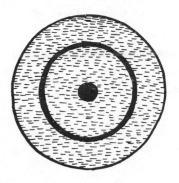

Fig. 50—*Design from an Apache hand-drum.*

drums have coloring on the sides of the frame also; the sides in A and B are maroon, and in C, light blue.

A typical design used on the rectangular drums of the Karok

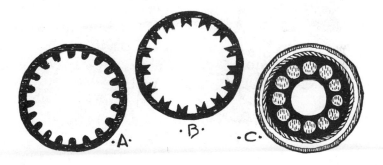

Fig. 51—*Indian drum designs from British Columbia.*

Indians of northern California is shown on page 64. The dark triangles are black and the sides are also black. There are four red triangles as indicated and the remainder of the drum is natural.

Alaskan Drum Designs.—When we come to Alaskan drums
we find the designs on the *inside* of the drumhead only, the
outside being unornamented — since these are single-headed
drums the design can be seen by looking into the rear. The
Alaskan drum designs usually consist of characteristic totem
symbols, two excellent examples of which are shown in Figure
52. The coloring is black, dark red, and green. The drum shown
in A has a design on the inside of the *drumframe* also, as indicated in the drawing.

Fig. 52—*Alaskan drum designs.*

Large Dance-Drums

CHAPTER IV

A FEW years ago we were camping in the Chippewa country when the dances were on, the occasion of the fiesta spirit being the presence of a delegation from a neighboring reservation of the same tribe. There was much celebration and, beginning at noon each day, constant dancing until early the next morning. Having spent one night and the next afternoon in the round dance-house, we became weary and left in the middle of the evening for our tent three miles away. But there was no sleeping, the big dance-drum booming as distinctly as if it were just over the hill, all night long. No sooner would we drift off in a moment of silence than the next dance would start, and "*Boom, boom,*" the big drum would shout.

No hand-drum could keep a council-ring of dancers under control with their bells jingling to the voices of the singers. Neither will it provide sufficient incentive for a large group of dancers in any type of modern dancing today. The big dance-drum, however, has volume sufficient to fill any hall or arena, for such is its purpose—the providing of rhythm for many dancers. As a percussion instrument of strength and volume for dancing groups, there is none better than the type of drum described in this chapter. The hand-drum discussed in the last chapter, if made without rattles, reminds one of the tenor-drum, and with rattles, the snare-drum, but the big dance-drum is the Indian counterpart of the bass-drum. However, as it is of heavier hide stretched tighter, and used with a hard beater, it gives forth a louder and more staccato sound than does the bass-drum of the bands today.

The enclosed dancing house of the woods-dwelling Indians is typically a round structure thirty or more feet in diameter, in the center of which is a circle of benches about five feet across, on which the drummers sit, from six to ten of them. Within this circle is the big dance-drum suspended from four upright poles which elevate it a few inches from the floor. The dancers move around the drummers, usually in a clockwise direction. The ten or so drummers, all wielding their beaters in unison, produce explosive boomings that fairly shake the rafters. Again one sometimes sees, although rarely, a square or rectangular dance-house, and in these the drum is located in the center also. Occasionally the dance arena is an exposed circle merely enclosed around the sides by a solid fence or wall of poles—six to eight feet high, with openings for passage ways to the east and west. Here, as in the round-house, the drum is enclosed in a circle of benches in the center, unless the ring is reserved for some special dance-society ceremony, in which case it may be located to one side of center. The dancing circle of the Plains Indians has much the same arrangement.

Today dancing drums are made by the Indians over large wooden tubs and appear as shown in Figure 53. In ancient days, when a finished drum was not available, the circle of drummers would hold a rawhide with one hand each and, stretching it between them, would slap it with the other hand. The Chippewas of long years past made dance-drums by driving a circle of split cedar poles into the ground, thus forming an immovable circular frame about two feet across and two feet high, the poles being so close together that they touched each other; over this the hide was stretched and laced to notches cut in the sticks. In more recent days their dance-drums were made by bending a cedar board about a foot in width into a hoop following the same method of bending described for making the narrow hand-drum frames in Chapter

III. Because of the difficulty of bending a wide and sufficiently heavy board, it was sometimes necessary to use two thin frames one placed around the outside of the other and bound to it as described for cheese-box hoop drums in Chapter III. While this method of bending a cedar frame is the ideal woodcraft way, it is by no means necessary for no better frame could be desired than the cedar wash-tub used by the Indians in recent years.

Huge tub-shaped dance-drums were used by many widely scattered tribes. To the woodland tribes the big dance-drum was the central object in the village and seemed to symbolize community spirit and solidarity. And whether among Chippewas, Menominees, Winnebagos, Sauk-Fox or other tribes of the north-central woods, these dance drums, both lay and sacred, were much alike in detail of construction and decoration. So, too, with the dance-drums of the neighboring Iowas. The same general type of drum appears also among the Dakotas—I once saw a huge Sioux drum of the tub type that measured three feet in diameter. Likewise, the Shoshoni and other tribes still farther to the westward used booming dance-drums of the general shape of a tub.

Among the woods-dwelling Indians the *powwow* or *everybody's drum* is the general dance drum, usable for any kind of commonplace dance where the rank and file of the tribal folk are present. *The dream-dance drum,* however, is reserved for the *dream dance,* that sacred and colorful religious ritual of Messianic nature that developed among the northern Woodland Indians at about the same time that the ghost dance was sweeping the Plains. The dream dance faintly resembles the ghost dance of the Plains and is thought by some to have elements of the latter in it.

These two types of drums are constructed in exactly the same way, the difference resting in the decorations.

THE POWWOW DRUM

Large and pretentious as they are, dance-drums are never-theless the easiest drums to construct, for the reason that a ready-made wash-tub serves the purpose of a frame, thus re-lieving us of the most difficult part of primitive drum-making —fashioning the frame.

The Tub Frame.—Secure from the hardware store a *cedar* wash-tub. Lard tubs, butter tubs, and the like can frequently be picked up for little or nothing but these are seldom made of cedar and consequently produce a drum that by comparison is definitely inferior in tone and resonance. *Insist on cedar.* Cedar wash-tubs are not as plentiful as they were a few years ago before the rise to popularity of galvanized tubs, but they are still made and any hardware store can secure them even if they do not carry them in stock. They are quite inexpensive.

Wooden tubs usually come in a variety of sizes, from a diameter of twenty inches, inside dimension, up to twenty-six inches. Any of the sizes may be used but the twenty-inch diameter is amply large and is recommended. A larger drum will produce but little more in volume, is more unwieldy, and increases the cost of the rawhide for drumheads.

All that needs to be done to the tub is to cut out the bottom. Draw a circle around the bottom two inches from the edge as shown in B, Figure 53, and cut out the bottom along this line with a key-hole saw. To get started with the sawing it will be necessary to bore a hole with a brace and bit large enough so that the point of the keyhole saw can be inserted. The two inches of bottom around the edge is necessary to furnish sup-port for the sides and prevent the tub from collapsing.

Wooden tubs usually have a wire or metal hoop around the sides. This will not be needed when the rawhide is in place, and should be removed for the sake of a neat drum.

Making the Drum.—Send to a manufacturer of rawhide products or drumheads for two pieces of hide for the two heads, specifying the purpose for which they are to be used. It is better to send the exact dimensions of the heads, ordering the circu-

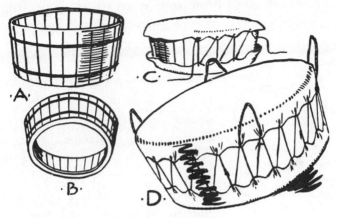

Fig. 53—*Making the Large Dance-Drum.*

lar pieces cut to size, thus securing no more hide than necessary. Measure the diameter of the top and of the bottom of the drum, then add six inches to each so that the hide will fold down the sides three inches; that is, if the top of the tub measures twenty-one inches, outside dimension, and the bottom nineteen inches, order two circular pieces of rawhide twenty-seven inches and twenty-five inches in diameter. Ask that one pound of rawhide scraps be thrown in for lacings. Good, strong rawhide for these large drumheads that are to receive heavy use will cost a little more than that for hand-drums, but one of these big dance-drums is well worth the expenditure.

Place the drumheads and scrap rawhide in water and leave for a full twenty-four hours. It is always better to soak drumheads in cold water for a long time, than to rush matters by softening them quickly in warm water.

Put the drumheads in place on the tub, stretch them tightly and tack temporarily to the sides of the tub, driving the tacks in just far enough to hold. The hides should be stretched just tight enough so that they are straight and smooth, do not sag, and vibrate with a soft drum tone when struck. Now, from the scrap rawhide, cut several long laces a full half inch in width, following the instructions for making laces on page 45 and illustrated in Figure 54. Next, cut a hole a half inch from the edge of the top rawhide, and directly below it a similar hole in the bottom drumhead, these holes being just large enough to slip the lacing through. Now cut similar holes every three inches around the edge of the top head, and directly under each a corresponding hole in the bottom head. Run the lacing through the top hole, down through the hole in the bottom head directly under it, then diagonally up to the next top hole, and so on, as shown in C. Continue this all around the drum. If the end of the thong is reached before the lacing is completed, tie to it another thong. The reason for placing the bottom holes directly under the upper ones is that a neater and more atractive job is produced thereby.

Fig. 54
Method of cutting lacings.

With the lacings all in place, withdraw the tacks and begin the tightening process. Go around the drum two or three times pulling the lacing tight at each hole, but being careful not to overdo the matter or the heads will be stretched too much. When finished tie the two ends of the lacing together where they meet.

Handles are tacked on the tub as shown in the drawing of the finished drum, D in Figure 53. The handles should not be tied to the rawhide in this type of drum—either tack them to the wood or bore holes through the sides of the tub and run them through. To make the handles, cut a string of wet rawhide one inch wide, twist it into a round thong, and tack in place. If the drum is hung by the handles while it dries, the handles will set up permanently in the position shown in D. The handles are four in number and should extend about two inches above the top of the drum.

Let the drum dry for a full twenty-four hours, following carefully the instructions given on page 49, and it will be ready to use.

Holders or racks for supporting the large dance-drum are described later in this chapter.

These drums call for hard beaters of the type discussed in Chapter VII.

Decorating the Powwow Drum

The drumhead should be colored immediately after the drum is finished and before the hide has dried. If it is desired to produce a highly ornamented tomtom on the order of the dream-dance drum, the complete description of that drum given later in this chapter should be read. The Chippewas, however, would decorate a powwow drum for ordinary dance purposes merely by painting the top solid red. Mix a little red paint powder (see page 78) with water, making a thin paste, and rub it with the fingers onto the top drumhead while the rawhide is still wet. Cover it solidly and evenly, but be careful not to extend the paint down onto the sides—the painting should end at the top edge of the drum. When the hide dries, the paint will be permanently fixed.

If carefully and neatly laced the drum will now present a very attractive appearance without further ornamentation. If desired, however, a skirt of cloth may be added, thus covering the sides. The beautiful skirt described for the dream-dance drum is the pinnacle of drum decoration, but such an elaborate effort with beading and all the other accessories is scarcely necessary—a simple skirt of colored cloth perhaps livened up with a few cloth scallops would be the Indian's way of decorating an ordinary powwow drum. In its simplest form the skirt consists of a piece of navy blue cloth, felt being preferred of the materials of reasonable price, tacked around the top of the drum and sewed at the ends so that the cloth adheres tightly to the sides. The skirt should hang down two inches below the bottom. Figure 55 shows a drum with a blue skirt, with an over skirt of red scallops of the same material at the top. Frequently one sees a powwow drum among the Indians with the skirt made of ordinary cotton cloth such as calico.

Fig. 55
Powwow Drum with Skirt.

A more elaborate skirt of felt or cotton cloth is shown in Figure 56. Three colors of cloth are used—red, yellow, and blue. The scalloped effect is obtained by placing one layer of cloth above another, each shorter than the one below it. The floral designs near the top are cut out of cloth and appliquéd.

We now have as serviceable a dance-drum as can be produced and one that will do heavy duty for many years. It lacks the beauty of the gorgeous dream-medicine drum but equals it in every other respect.

Other Materials for Powwow Drumframes

In case a cedar washtub cannot be obtained, use a *lard tub* picked up at a grocery store or any similar wooden tub regardless of the kind of wood from which it is made. Aside from cedar, there is not much choice among woods. Or, a small drum of this general type can be made from a *wooden bucket,* an item that grocery stores usually have at hand. A dance-drum can also be made from *cheese-box* wood by taking apart four boxes and placing the four frames over each other, thus making

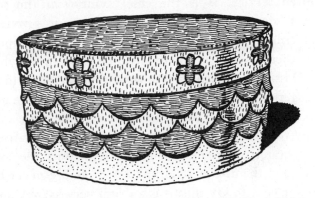

Fig. 56—*Chippewa Powwow Drum with Cloth Skirt.*

four thicknesses of wood which must be laced together as described on page 72. The use of cheese-boxes is not recommended, however, because the frame will be too small in diameter, flimsy, and inclined to warp. Wooden tubs are too easy to obtain to waste time and rawhide on cheese-boxes.

THE CHIPPEWA DREAM-DANCE DRUM

The most beautiful drum made in this country, barring none by white man or Indian, is the dream-dance drum. A good specimen of this gorgeous instrument is a sight to behold, especially appealing to those whose eyes are accustomed to Indian art, but of such general beauty that all who see it will respond. To the Chippewas and neighboring tribes of the same culture area, its beauty is but incidental to the powerful medicine qualities it possesses.

It is impossible to determine which is the more sacred drum, the dream-dance one or the water-drum, the latter being a true

medicine drum. Each is considered among the Woodland
Indians as possessing a rare potency all its own and each is
unique to the ceremonies for which it is reserved. The dream-
dance drum is as central to the dream-dance as is the altar to
the church service. It is the chief symbol in the so-called
Chippewa "drum religion"—it is the *gift drum* given by one
band or tribe to another as a token of friendship and peace
between them (peace is an important factor in the drum religion). On such occasions one of these elaborately ornamented
drums together with all the trappings, including peace pipe and
tobacco, is presented to the other band or tribe with a dancing
ceremony that lasts several days. Since the Indians are exceed-
ingly reluctant to discuss their sacred drums, the symbolic
significance of the dreamer's drum will probably never be fully
known—suffice it to say that it is a drum very sacred, and most
carefully guarded.

The dream-dance drum differs from the big dance-drum for
general use just described chiefly in its ornamentation. While
a person making and decorating a dance-drum for use today
may not be at all concerned about duplicating a dream-dance
drum, yet if the general type of ornamentation is followed, a
gorgeous instrument will result that will grace any dancing
stage or setting where primitive atmosphere and beauty are
desired.

In construction, the dream-dance drum is exactly like the
powwow drum described in the foregoing pages with one ex-
ception—there is a bell inside. Unless a three-inch open bell can
be secured of the type that sometimes was added to a string
of sleigh bells in years past, a turkey bell obtainable from any
large hardware store should be used. Before putting the hide
over the wooden tub, bore two small holes on opposite sides
of the tub each a half inch from the top, and suspend the bell
on a thong of buckskin or a string tied to these holes as shown

in Figure 57 which illustrates a cross section of the tub. The string should sag two or three inches to give the bell a chance to swing.

Fig. 57—*Bell suspended inside the Dream-dance Drum.*

The four handles must be carefully placed: two of them are located exactly at each end of the yellow stripe going across the drum described in the following paragraph; the other two are placed midway between these two. The handles are nailed to the wood and then run through the slits in the cloth skirt after it is attached to the drum. The handles should extend two and one-half inches above the top of the drum and care should be taken to see that each is of exactly the same length.

Painting the Dream-dance Drum.—Both the top and bottom drumheads are painted, each with the same design, so arranged that each element in the design on the bottom drumhead is directly under the same element on the top hide. Figure

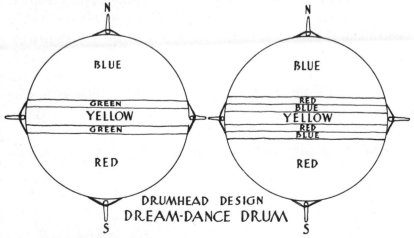

DRUMHEAD DESIGN
DREAM-DANCE DRUM

58 shows the design. Directly across the center is a yellow stripe one inch wide, and along each side of it and touching it is a one-quarter inch green stripe. The drumhead to one side of this stripe is painted solid red and to the other side solid blue.

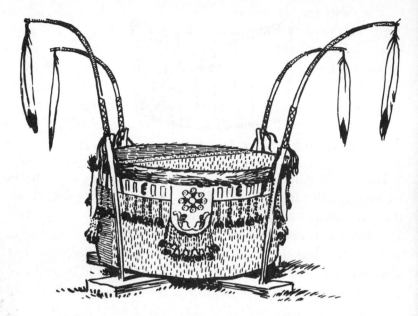

Fig. 58—*The Chippewa Dream-dance Drum in hanger.*

This same design appears on some of the very small medicine hand-drums used by medicine men in treating the sick (see C, Figure 23). The dream-dance drum is always placed so that the yellow stripe goes east and west, with the blue side to the north and the red side to the south. The stripe represents the path of the sun, the red the brightness and warmth to the south, and the blue the darker heavens to the north. Sometimes the yellow band is edged with quarter-inch red and blue stripes on either side, instead of the green edgings, as shown in the accompanying diagram.

Aside from any symbolic meaning it may have, this drumhead design is unusually satisfying—dignified, reserved, and appropriate for a richly decorated drum such as this. Instructions regarding the paint and methods of applying it are given on page 78.

The Skirt for the Dream-Dance Drum.—It is in the adornment of the skirt that the drum achieves its chief splendor. Red and blue is the main color scheme of the dream-dance drum and both the drumheads and the skirt are in these colors. The skirt on the side of the drum beneath the blue area is made of blue wool cloth, whereas that beneath the red area consists of red wool cloth, the two colors of cloth being sewed together below the ends of the yellow stripe. The skirt is fitted snugly to the sides of the drum and extends down two inches below it. The Indians would use for this the deep navy blue cloth and red cloth issued by the government to the Indians in years past, known as Indian list cloth. It is heavy, rich-looking wool cloth from which the Plains Indians made clothing and blankets after the passing of the buffalo. Any wool cloth in rich navy blue and deep red may be used. An inexpensive substitute which will stand up with good care is found in felt. Contrary to popular opinion the men of the Woods-dwelling and Plains Indians did not run to gaudiness in the materials from which clothing was made, but rather preferred to achieve ornamentation in the beading and trinkets attached to it. The Chippewa men in particular favored deep navy blue or black for dancing clothes, resorting occasionally to deep maroon. Similarly, they preferred skirts for their dance-drums in rich, deep colors, relying on the beading and other additions for added attractiveness.

To determine the size of the pieces of cloth needed, take one-half the circumference of the drum for the length, and the depth of the drum plus two inches for the width. Two pieces of this size will be required, one in blue and the other in red.

Now let us consider the hangings and trappings that are attached to the cloth skirt. The materials needed are twenty-four thimbles, two hundred and forty round wooden beads one-half inch in diameter in red, blue, and yellow; one hundred and forty-four transparent glass beads one-quarter inch wide; a beaded band sixty-eight inches long, and four elaborate beaded pieces of special design; a quantity of beaver fur, and of red and blue yarn.

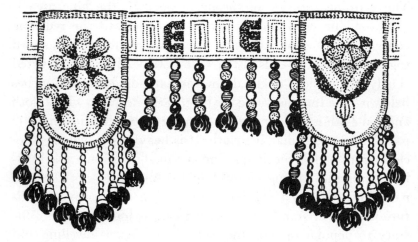

Fig. 59—*Beaded design on Chippewa Dream-dance Drum.*

Around the top of the drum is a strip of beaver fur an inch and a half wide tacked through the cloth to the wood; in case beaver is not available any fur may be substituted. Directly under the fur and touching it, a beaded band goes all the way around the drum, this being two and one-half inches wide and sixty-eight inches long; its placement is shown in Figure 58, and the detailed design in Figure 59. In producing an authentic drum the detail of this beading is important: The background is white with the designs in red and blue. It will be noted from the illustration that there is a figure resembling a capital E—

this is in red outlined with a single row of blue beads; this figure is an inch and five-eighths high and one and one-sixteenth inches wide. Between these figures are two rectangular-shaped figures an inch and a half high and seven-eighths inch wide. These consist of two rectangles in light blue, one inside the other, separated by a double row of white beads; in the center of the inner one is one row of red beads around which is a single row of white beads. Near each edge of the beaded band is a line of dark blue beads.

Next there are four large beaded pieces to be added, placed as in Figures 58 and 59. These are tacked over the top of the beaded band so that the top of each piece is even with the top of the band. There are two designs used in making these pieces, two pieces being made in each design; those with the design at the left, Figure 59 are placed on the *blue* side of the drum and those containing the figure at the right are put on the *red* side. The exact placement of these beaded pieces is best visualized by referring to the position of the drum in the four standards or uprights in Figure 58: two of the standards are at the ends of the yellow line across the drumhead, and the other two are at the ends of an imaginary line across the center at right angles to this yellow line, thus placing one midway of the red half and the other midway of the blue half; the beaded pieces are then placed halfway between these standards.

The detail of the beaded pieces is shown in Figure 59. They are four and one-half inches wide and six and one-half inches high, but since they are edged with blue cloth one-quarter inch wide, the actual beaded area is reduced in size accordingly. The background is white with the floral designs in blue, red and a very little yellow. This beading is sewed onto a heavy cloth foundation.

It will be noted that there are nine hangings of large beads at the bottom of each of these beaded pieces. Each of the two outer hangings consists of six round, half-inch wooden beads in blue, red, and yellow, and the six strings between them of six round, transparent glass beads one-quarter inch wide. Below the beads on each string is a thimble as indicated in Figure 59 (sometimes a piece of tin turned into a cone shape as shown in Figure 118 is used instead of the thimble). Below the thimble is a little tassel of red and blue yarn; each strand of yarn in the tassel is but one-half inch long, and the result is a round fluffy ball.

To the beaded band going around the top of the drum, strings of wood beads are attached as shown, each consisting of six half-inch round beads in red, blue, and yellow, at the bottom of which is the little tassel of red and blue yarn. These are placed an inch apart, thirty-two strings being needed in all.

A lot of work and no small amount of materials go into such a drum as this, but the result is a gorgeous and impressive instrument. Its effect as an ornament is hard to visualize until seen.

The dream-dance drum is suspended in the specially prepared standards shown in Figure 58, the details of which are discussed under the heading, "Dance-drum Hangers."

Ornamented drums of this type call for drumsticks with curved ends and covered with beaver fur and ribbon as described on page 155.

DANCE-DRUM HANGERS

A rich, full, booming tone becomes possible only when a drum is suspended in the air. It is then free, vibrant, with a light, airy quality, suggestive of and inspiring the dance. In contact with the ground or some other object, the tone is flat, muffled, restrained—a dull thump, as though the voice were imprisoned within the object the drum touches. Hand-drums can be easily held free in the hand, but the larger type must be so supported that no object touches it at any point other than at the handles.

A large dance-drum must be suspended in such a way that the top is parallel to the floor, thus spreading the broad drumhead before the drummer so that he can apply the beater freely while watching the dancers. First let us consider the woods-Indian method of supporting the dance-drum, then a modern method that may be more practical today.

Fig. 60—*Simple hanger for a large dance-drum.*

Powwow Drum Hangers.—A simple hanger for a powwow drum is made by the Indians by merely driving four poles in the ground, each with a notch cut in the top to receive the handle, as shown in Figure 60. These are just high enough so as to suspend the drum a few inches off the ground, thus elevating it at a convenient height so that it can be played while seated on a low bench or kneeling on the ground. The poles should not touch the drumframe as it hangs.

Dream-Dance Drum Hangers.—It is only appropriate that the beautifully ornamented dream-dance drum should have an elaborate hanger such as that shown in Figure 58. These curved stick hangers are always employed for elaborately decorated dance-drums, but unfortunately they are a little difficult to construct.

Four holes are made in the ground six inches deep into which the four curved uprights are inserted, but since the drum will often be used indoors today, a frame of two-by-fours may be made with holes in which to insert the standards as shown in

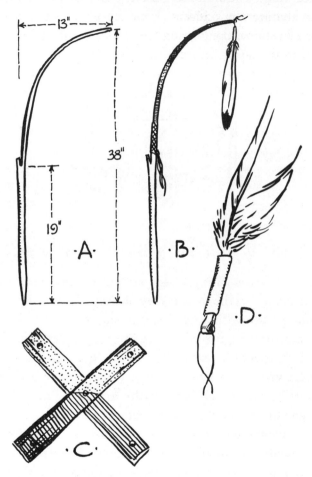

Fig. 61—*Detail of hanger for the Dream-dance Drum.*

C, Figure 61. In case the uprights are to be inserted into the ground the sticks from which they are to be made should be four feet six inches long, but if the two-by-four frame is to be used, a length of only four feet will be needed. The dimensions shown in Figure 61 assume that the latter will be the case. The poles are of black ash and should be whittled to shape before they are bent. The notch is nineteen inches up as shown; the stick in the section below it is larger than that above it, and is oblong in shape, the long diameter being one and one-quarter inches and the short diameter three-quarters inch, the extreme bottom being narrowed down to fit a five-eighths-inch hole. Above the notch the stick is round, measuring three-quarters in diameter except at the top end which is tapered down to one-half inch.

When finished the four sticks are placed side by side and lashed together securely, then placed under water and allowed to soak for twenty-four hours. Thus soaked they will bend easily—the best way to accomplish this is to drive two stout, short poles in the ground a foot apart, place the ends of the bound sticks against one pole and pull the sticks against the other pole until the desired amount of curve has been produced, then drive another pole in the ground near the other end to hold them in this position. After remaining thus for twenty-four hours or until thoroughly dry, the curve will be permanently fixed. Figure 61 indicates the distance the poles should be bent.

Smooth up the curved sticks with sandpaper and they are ready for the beading. The beads are merely strung on a thread and wrapped around the stick so as to cover it solidly—there should be yellow beads for a distance of six inches at the end, then four-inch sections of each of the following colors in turn: blue, green, red, white. Below the white beading and just above the notch there is a four-inch section that is wrapped with one-inch strips of the blue and red cloth used in the skirt.

At the end of each curved stick a white-and-black tipped

eagle feather is attached. The quill ends of the feathers are prepared with a leather strip covered with colored wool cloth as shown in D, Figure 61, following the same plan as used in preparing feathers for a headdress. Two are wrapped with blue cloth for the blue side of the drum, and two with red for the red side. They are then tied to the end of the stick with string so as to hang down and blow in the breeze. Occasionally one sees one of these drum hangers with the eagle feathers set up on top of the sticks so that they stand erect. In this case the feather is attached in a little wooden tube as for use on a roach and the tube attached to the top of the curved standard. The more common practice is to allow the feathers to hang down as in Figure 61.

The two-by-fours in the bottom frame are twenty-seven and a half inches long, each having a section cut out at the center one inch deep and four inches wide so that the two pieces will fit together without the use of nails, and can be separated for convenient storing when not in use. A hole is bored two and three-quarters inches from each end to receive the upright. Half of this two-by-four frame is painted blue for the blue half of the drum and the other half red for the red side of the drum.

If the hangers are made to the dimensions stated, and the handles are of such length that they extend two and one-half inches above the drum, the top of the drum should hang at the proper distance above the floor—sixteen to seventeen inches.

Remember that the dream-dance drum should be placed in the hanger so that the yellow stripe goes east and west, the blue side is to the north, and the red to the south.

Modern Drum Supports.—For use in dancing groups, gymnasiums, and camps today a rack will be preferred that elevates the drum to such a height that it can be used while the drummer is standing. Although in no respect comparable in appearance to the Indian supports of curved sticks just described, a convenient, movable hanger of this type is shown in Figure 62. If made of cedar or other soft wood, it will be light in weight and easily moved. There are notches cut in the sticks near the top in which the drum handles are hooked, allowing the drum to hang free and unhampered. The exact height of these notches will have to be determined by experimentation, the drummer endeavoring to place the top of the drum just at the waist-line.

Fig. 62—*High hanger for a powwow drum.*

Drums of the Log or Barrel Type

CHAPTER V

ALL of the drums described thus far in this book are broader than they are deep, but we now come to the type that is longer than it is broad—the log or barrel-type drum for which the Indians of the southwest areas are noted, so called because it is built over a hollow log that has somewhat the proportions of a keg. These drums, often called tombés in the Southwest, are picturesque always and possess a characteristic and very appealing tomtom tone.

This type of drum is better known and more commonly seen about the country today than the hand-drums and large dance-drums discussed in preceding chapters, owing to the fact that shoddy imitations of the Indian-made ones have been commercialized and sold in tourist shops and novelty stores. In the old days their use was confined largely to the Southwest tribes, other tribes making but little use of a deep drum. There are exceptions, of course, the Assiniboine log-drum, referred to later in this chapter, being an example of the appearance of this style among the Plains Indians, and the Seneca log-drum of its use in the eastern area.

Here is the drum of the mesa and desert country—the dance-drum and the war-drum of the Pueblos, Hopis, Navajos, and Apaches. Let us first describe just how these picturesque folks of the Southwest fashioned their tombés and how we may construct them according to authentic Indian methods; then we shall take up the matter of making similar drums out of materials easy to pick up anywhere.

THE SOUTHWEST INDIAN LOG-DRUM

Hollow cottonwood logs are in great demand among the Indians of the Southwest states, for cottonwood is the traditional material from which drums are made. How unfortunate it is that white cedar does not grow in the Pueblo country, for if it were to be had, cottonwood would surely have long since lost its popularity. True enough, cottonwood is easy to work and does produce a drum light in weight and of delightful tone, but the contrast is startling when such a drum is played alongside one of similar shape made from the white cedar of the North — vibrant, light, airy, the cedar tone instantly and definitely is labeled as superior. Its sound is scarcely characteristic of the traditional cottonwood drum, but it is unquestionably a better instrument. Cottonwood has been so extensively used for the very good reason that it is available to these Indians.

Many big cedars were taken down in the Lake Superior lumbering country before the uncracked hollow butt was found that now is the frame of my big log drum, measuring thirty inches deep with drumheads of thin rawhide twenty-one inches across. When struck its resounding boom is followed by many overtones reminding one of a huge organ, which continue to vibrate audibly for more than fifteen seconds afterward. Its tone and its echoing reverberations are without equal in my experience. I showed this to a primitive Pueblo Indian once, and no sooner did he strike it than his face became radiant and, entranced, he played it and experimented with it for an hour. Maintaining it was the finest drum he had ever seen, he was mystified as to what produced this superiority over the drums of his people. In its shape and decoration, it was true to the ways of his tribe, but its tone was different and definitely better. The secret rested in the wood—cedar, not cottonwood.

Making the Log Frame.—Like the Indians, we must make the drumframe from the materials to be found in the section of the country in which we find ourselves. If where white cedar grows, by all means use it; if where cottonwood is available, it is excellent; otherwise use very soft wood that can be easily worked. Since we must have a *hollow* log, we cannot always exercise much choice in the matter but are forced to use almost any hollow log of soft wood that happens to be available. Large white cedars are more often hollow than not.

The outer shell of the hollow log must be solid and uncracked. The small checks that appear in the end of any dry log make no difference at all, but there can be no large cracks. If a live tree is taken down for the purpose, the shell is apt to crack badly shortly after it is cut—this is especially true of cedar cut in the swampy regions in which it thrives. To forestall such a happening, take along a bucket of paint, and as soon as the tree is dropped, saw off the section desired for the drum and immediately paint the sawed ends. The paint will prevent splitting while the wood dries out. Often we are fortunate enough to find an old log lying on the ground that has a hollow center but with sides solid and uncracked.

The drum should be a little less than twice as long as it is wide. For example, a drum twelve inches in diameter should be about twenty to twenty-two inches deep.

The tools needed are a mallet, large chisel and gouge, drawknife, and jackknife. The mallet may be easily made by cutting off a five-inch piece from a three-inch hardwood limb, boring a hole in the side, and inserting a handle of the thickness of a broomstick, as shown in Figure 63.

Set the log on end as in A, Figure 63, and applying the mallet to the chisel and gouge, cut the wood from the hollow center. At first the wood may be knocked out very rapidly, but as the edge is neared the work must be done slowly and cautiously for fear of splitting the frame or cutting too deeply and thus making it too thin. The outside of the log should likewise be cleaned and smoothed up, this with the aid of a drawknife. The log should be pulled down to a thin shell, not over a half inch in thickness—the thinner the better; a free, resonant tone results if the sides are thin, a dull and muffled sound if they are thick. When the work on the log is all completed, round off the top and bottom edges a little with a knife to prevent their cutting the rawhide.

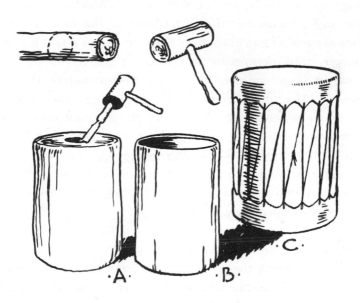

Fig. 63—*Making the Southwest Log Drum.*

It makes no difference if the log is not perfectly symmetrical. One must accept the log as it comes, however lopsided it may be, and the original contour should be maintained rather than work it into a circular shape. Some of the most attractive of log tombés are quite irregular.

In case there is a knot-hole in the log it should be plugged up with a round plug whittled to the exact shape of the hole and glued in place. If a minor split should accidentally occur, it can be repaired by filling the crack with a little liquid solder.

Making the Drum.—Let us assume that we now have a log frame prepared which is a little less than twice as long as it is wide, from which all possible wood has been removed, leaving a thin shell such as that shown in B, Figure 63. Further, let us assume that the rawhide for the drumheads has been soaking in water for twenty-four hours. The drumhead should be large enough to extend down the sides a considerable distance as shown in C, Figure 63: if the diameter of the drum is twelve inches a circle of rawhide should be cut twenty-two inches in diameter, thus permitting it to extend down the sides five inches; in larger or smaller drums approximately the same proportion should be maintained. Stretch the hide across the top just tight enough so that it does not sag and tack it temporarily to the sides of the log. Then tack the other head in place in the same way. Remember to keep the hide wet by rubbing water on it with the hand at proper intervals.

There are two common methods of lacing the drumheads together, one as effective as the other so far as producing a good drum is concerned, but each giving a different appearance to the drum when decorations in keeping with the lacing pattern are added. Perhaps the more popular method is that shown in C, Figure 63: Note that every other thong is perpendicular to the ground, whereas the thong in between is at an angle. The other type is that shown in A, Figure 65—it will be observed that each thong is at an angle. Let us consider the style shown in Figure 63 first:

Cut small holes in the edge of each drumhead, placing these three-eighths of an inch from the edge and four inches apart, and being sure that the holes in the bottom hide are directly under those in the top. From the rawhide trimmings cut long thongs one-quarter inch wide following the method described on page 45 and illustrated in C, Figure 7. Run one of these thongs through the holes in the drumheads, lacing the two heads together following the lacing pattern shown in C. When the end of the thong is reached, tie another to it. With the lacing completed, withdraw the tacks and proceed to tighten the thongs, pulling gently at each hole, going around the drum two or three times tightening a little more each time. Then tie the ends of the thong together. To make the handles cut two strips of rawhide one inch wide and twelve inches long, twist each into a circular thong, and tie to the lacing (Figure 66), one at the top and the other directly under it at the bottom. Hang the drum up to dry for at least twenty-four hours, following the instructions on page 49.

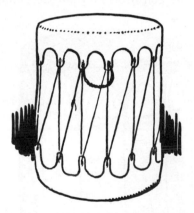

Fig. 64—*A common style of lacing and trimming the rawhide.*

The completed drum now appears as in C, Figure 63. The drum may be left in this condition, but it will take on much in the way of attractiveness if the hide between lacings is cut to the semicircular shape shown in Figure 64. This can be quickly done with a pair of small scissors while the hide is still wet. The height of the semicircular cut is equal to the distance be-

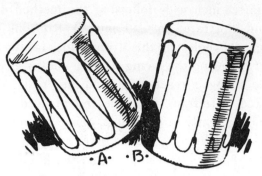

Fig. 65—*Other methods of lacing log drums.*

tween the lacings. Another method often used, although not so common as the semicircular design, is to cut the hide to a point as shown in Figure 73.

The second of the common methods of lacing, that in which

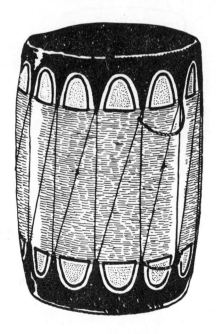

Fig. 66—*A typical Pueblo log drum.*

all the thongs are at an angle and none perpendicular, is shown in A, Figure 65. Cut the holes in the top drumhead four inches apart, then cut the holes in the bottom hide the same distance apart but so placed that each is directly below the middle of the uncut sections of the top hide. Then proceed with the lacing as usual.

A third but less prevalent method of lacing is shown in B, Figure 65. Short thongs are used, tied to the drumheads at the top and bottom. Special caution must be taken to see that all of these thongs are given the same amount of tension or the drumhead may be pulled to one side by the greater pressure of the tighter thongs.

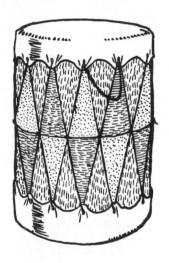

Fig.67—*An attractive method of lacing.*

Another lacing style that produces a very beautiful drum and lends itself exceptionally well to decoration is shown in Figure 67. A study of the picture will indicate the method: two thongs are used; the first one is run through every other hole, and then the second thong is run through the remaining holes. When the lacing is completed a thong is run around the middle of the drum as shown, being looped around each intersection of the upright lacings.

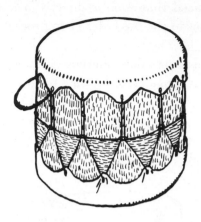

Fig. 68—*An Apache Drum.*

An Apache method of lacing is shown in Figure 68. This is rare and not particularly successful in producing tight drumheads.

Still another style of lacing can be clearly followed from the illustration in Figure 69. Since this is more difficult and produces a less attractive tombé than any of the other methods,

Fig. 69

it is recorded here merely because it is sometimes seen, although rarely, among the drums of the Southwest Indians.

The final task in completing the drum is to bore a tiny hole through the side not over a quarter of an inch in diameter, this being placed midway between the two ends. The presence of this hole is required more by tradition than by utility, but it is pretty sure to be present in a genuine old-time drum.

The drumheads should be painted while the rawhide is still wet although the decorating of the wood should be postponed until the heads have dried. Detailed directions for decorating are given later in this chapter.

Southwest tombes are most effective when used with one of the soft drumsticks described in Chapter VII, "Drumsticks."

A Plains Indian Log-Drum

While drums built over hollow logs were not common outside the southwest area, yet there were other tribes that made

Fig. 70—*A Plains Indian upright drum.*
Fig. 71—*A Southwest drum hanger.*

some use of them. For example, the Assiniboines of the northern Plains used a drum somewhat on this order as illustrated in Figure 70. This is a very tall and thin drum, the hollow log being about thirty inches long, smaller at the top than at the bottom. There is only one head to the drum, the bottom being entirely open. The drumhead is laced to the logs through holes burnt through the wood, using the method of lacing shown in Figure 13, and described on page 58. While this method would produce a drum of good tone yet it is scarcely comparable to the more finished drums of the Southwest Indians as described in the preceding pages.

Pueblo Drum Hangers

Like all drums the hollow-log tombé must be held free from contact with solid objects if its tone is to be rich, full, and airy. A drum of average size can easily be held in the hand but the task is made easier by the simple device of the Pueblo Indians shown in Figure 71. Cut a stick in the woods that has a branch off to one side which, when trimmed off four inches from the main branch, will form the hook as illustrated. The upright is run through the lower handle, and the upper handle slipped over the hook.

The bottom of this hanger is placed on the ground and the stick held upright with one hand, leaving the other free to handle the thumper.

DECORATING THE SOUTHWEST DRUM

The log-style tombé lends itself admirably to painted decoration, striking effects being obtainable by alternating colors in the sections between the lacings and by other color patterns. However rough and crude the appearance of the drum may be when it is finished, a little paint in proper Indian design turns it into a picturesque, and often beautiful, primitive instrument.

Painting the Log and Drumheads

The instructions given on page 78 for painting hoop-drums apply equally to log-style tombés with respect to type of paint used and method of application. The rawhide should be painted either with a dry paint powder mixed with enough water to form a thin paste or with liquid show-card paint. The paint should be applied after the hide has dried just enough so that the coloring will not run.

For the log frame liquid show-card paint is strongly recommended because of its refined coloring. House paint should never be used on a drum. After the show-card paint has been applied to the wood it should be covered with a fixative sold for use on watercoloring at any art store. This will preserve the paint, protect it against chipping off, and prevent it from spotting when water touches it. The result obtained by using show-card paint and the fixative is similar to the effect seen on Southwest Indian-made drums painted with cruder materials. If paint powder mixed with water is used on the wood, it should be treated with fixative also.

Designs for Southwest Log Drums

The drumheads of the Southwest drums are characteristically black, sometimes solid black and sometimes with a small spot of another color added in the center. Occasionally one sees a drumhead in a vivid color but the traditional custom is to use a dark shade, usually black, on the rawhide, and to rely on bright colors on the wooden sides of the drum to give the instrument attractiveness. The type of decoration depends somewhat on the style of lacing used on the drum. That is, a drum in which every other lacing is perpendicular as in Figure 64 lends itself to a different color pattern than that in which all the lacings are at an angle as in A, Figure 65. Let us describe first the designs for the type of drum in which every other lacing is perpendicular, this being the most characteristic type.

An authentic, traditional tombé design is shown in Figure 66, this being drawn from a very delightful drum from the Santa Domingo Pueblo. It will be noted that the drumheads and the rawhide extensions from them down the sides are solid black. The main body of the log frame is solid red in a dark shade. The semicircular spots around the edge of the rawhide giving the scalloped effect are first painted solid white, then the half-inch black line is applied near the edge as shown in Figure 66; in the center of the white area within this line there is a semicircular spot of yellow following the outline of the cut rawhide. This combination of colors if put on in two coats of paint and brightened with a little fixative produces a striking yet reserved and dignified drum.

Another good design is shown in D, Figure 72. It will be noted that the rawhide extending down the sides is black and that there is a two-inch black spot in the middle of the drumhead, whereas the rest of the drumhead is a medium shade of green. The solid area on the sides of the log is pure white and the semicircular spots are red set off from the white by a half-inch black line. The lacings across the white section are unpainted.

On the drum shown in A, Figure 72, the drumheads and the rawhide extending down the sides are solid black as shown. The triangular areas pointing up from the bottom are blue edged with white, whereas the triangular areas extending downward are red. There is a half-inch white line edging the rawhide around the semicircular sections.

Still another beautiful design is shown in C, Figure 72. The drumheads are black with a three-inch red spot in the center, and the rawhide extending down the sides from the drumheads is black. The wide stripe around the middle of the drum is red,

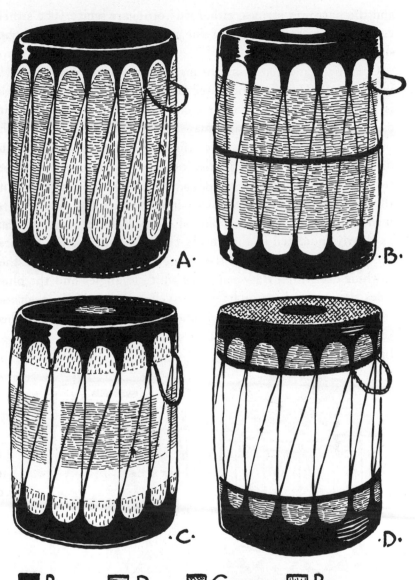

·A· ·B· ·C· ·D·

■ BLACK ▤ RED ▩ GREEN ▦ BLUE

Fig. 72—*Pueblo drum designs.*

and the narrower stripes, either side of it, are white. The semi-circular spots at the edge of the rawhide are a medium-light shade of blue.

One of the most striking drums in these pages is illustrated in A, Figure 73. It will be noted that the rawhide on the sides is cut to a triangular rather than a semicircular shape, but essentially the same design may be used regardless of which of these two styles of rawhide trimming the drum happens to have. The drumheads and the rawhide extending down the sides from them are black with a yellow spot in the center of the drumhead about three inches in diameter, and a tiny half-inch yellow spot near the point of each of the black triangles, as clearly indicated in Figure 73. The solid sides of the log are a light shade of blue and the triangular sections beneath the rawhide are white. Between these white triangles and the blue sides there is a three-quarter inch yellow line edged on either side with a quarter-inch black line. The lacing down the sides remains uncolored. If good colors are used this will be a delightful, refreshing drum.

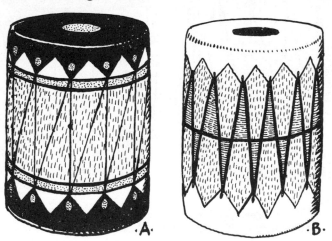

Fig. 73—*Southwest Indian drum designs.*

Coming now to the drums made with all lacings at an angle rather than perpendicular, we find in B, Figure 73 an unusually effective type of decoration. The drumheads and the extensions down the sides from them are pure white with a two-inch black spot in the center. There is a quarter-inch black stripe directly around the center of the log. The triangles pointing upward and downward from this line as shown are a medium red edged with quarter-inch black line. The areas between these triangles are a medium shade of blue. This is a striking drum.

Another drum with diagonal lacings is shown in B, Figure 72. The drumheads are black with a two-inch white spot in the middle. The sides are solid red with a three-eighths inch black line around the center as shown. The semicircular spots are white set off from the red with quarter-inch black lines.

The drum with the special diagonal lacing shown in Figure 67 lends itself admirably to many schemes of decoration. The colors in the pattern shown are blue, yellow, and red. The rawhide is uncolored.

While these designs and colorings are recorded from fine Indian drums of the Southwest, the colors may be changed to suit one's taste and the various designs combined in several ways. It is necessary to remember, however, that the authentic Indian type of decoration must be utilized if a drum is to be produced that will have a characteristic appearance and will ring true in the estimation of those who know. This being the case, liberties in combining the designs and creating new patterns should be taken only after careful study and thorough familiarity with the authentic ones here given.

Keg drums and other types from improvised materials suggested later in this chapter should be painted with the same designs recommended for the log drums. So decorated, they will look the part and belie the "civilized" materials from which they are made.

DRUMS FROM IMPROVISED MATERIALS

Let us now turn our attention to the making of drums of the log or barrel type from materials which can be picked up in any locality. Needless to say these should be a second choice to a hollow log, but they do offer excellent opportunities for the making of drums in schools, clubs, camps, and the like.

These materials are of the following types, each of which will be described in turn: (1) kegs, (2) wooden buckets, (3) tin cans, (4) cardboard cartons, (5) flower pots, (6) bulk cocoa cartons.

In the event that rawhide cannot be obtained, one of the substitutes described on page 29 may be used on these drums.

Keg Drums

The nearest thing in shape and size to the Southwest hollow-log tombé is an ordinary keg. A nail keg will make an excellent drum which when finished and decorated will take on all of the characteristic appearances of an authentic tombé and will be rather hard to distinguish from one when viewed at a sufficient distance so that the staves cannot be seen. Pickle kegs, wine kegs, cider kegs and similar water-tight kegs may also be used but they are not as satisfactory as a nail keg, owing to the fact that their sides are so thick and heavy, and so tightly fitted that a muffled, restraining tone results. If a nail-keg drum is made with the same care that would be used in making a hollow log drum a satisfying tombé is certain to result.

Remove the bottom of the keg and also the wires or metal hoops which surround it in the middle, leaving only the hoops at the extreme top and bottom. A quick and easy drum may be made by merely tacking the hide to the sides of the drum, but a more authentic appearance and better tone will result if the hide is laced just as in making the Southwest tombé described earlier in this chapter. Smooth up the sides with sandpaper and fill up any wide cracks with plastic wood. Bore the little quarter-inch hole which Indian tradition demands be present in every drum, and paint the drum with one of the interesting designs already described and illustrated.

A mammoth drum of this type may be made over a sugar barrel or other light barrel of similar type.

Wooden-Bucket Drums

An excellent drum may be made from one of the wooden buckets which grocery stores usually have on hand and which they are glad to dispose of after the contents have been emptied. Remove the bottom and apply the drumhead by lacing as described for the authentic Indian drums earlier in this chapter.

Tin-Can Drums

The ever-present tin can offers an excellent source of drum-frame for children's music and dancing classes in schools, and for clubs and camps. The *gallon vegetable cans* have approximately the right proportions, as do also the pound and half-pound *tobacco cans, coffee cans, cookie cans, popcorn cans,* and *lard pails,* any and all of which offer the opportunity for delightful drum projects that will arouse the enthusiasm of any group of children. The one-hundred-pound lard can is excellent for a large drum—your grocer will be glad to save you one.

Remove the bottom of the can or pail with a can-opener. The drumheads may be attached either by wrapping a thong of wet hide around as in B, Figure 74, or by lacing according to the authentic method shown in C, the latter producing a drumhead that will remain tight for a longer period than will the former. If rawhide cannot be found for the drumheads, use one of the substitutes recommended on page 29.

The tin-can drums are painted in exactly the same way as the log drums, but care must be taken to cover the tin completely since any uncovered spots, however tiny they may be,

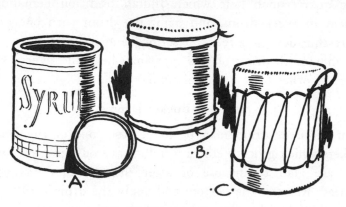

Fig. 74—*Tin-can drums.*

will reflect the light and make their presence glaringly apparent. When properly painted one can scarcely tell, by looking at it, that there is a tin can within.

Cardboard Carton Drums

The round cardboard cartons in which ice cream is packed offer another excellent source of frames for small drums for

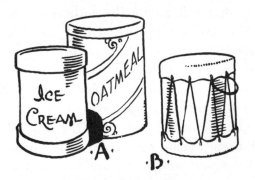

Fig. 75—*Drums from cardboard cartons.*

children's use, as do also the round boxes in which oatmeal, salt, and other groceries are sold. Secure the largest ones possible, cut out the bottoms and proceed just as described for the tin-can and other drums above. These are shown in Figure 75.

Flower-Pot Drums

Drums made from flower-pots have only one head, of course. These drums can be made in five minutes since the hide is not laced but merely tied by wrapping a wet rawhide thong around the pot beneath the ridge as shown in B, Figure 76. The flower-pot takes paint well and can be interestingly decorated.

Drums from Cocoa Cartons

No better frame for a tombé can be found than one of the round wooden cartons in which bulk cocoa is packed. Ask your grocer about these. They are thin, light in weight, and of the right proportions. Lace the rawhide over them as described earlier in this chapter.

Other Materials for Drumframes

A round composition waste-basket will make a good drum. One of the large galvanized cans sold at hardware stores as refuse containers can be turned into a drumframe by removing

Fig. 76—*Flower-pot drums.*

the bottom. But enough has been said to indicate that such a wide variety of materials is available that no one need want for a frame. Once one has made a drum or two he will spot and pick up suitable objects in all sorts of unexpected places.

Water-Drums

CHAPTER VI

EVERYONE is familiar with the fact that sound carries farther on a rainy day than a clear one. Similarly the voices of swimmers and paddlers can be heard much more distinctly and for far greater distances than would be the case if they were on land. Herein rests the secret of the water-drum—the presence of the water within gives the sound far greater carrying power than a dry drum possesses.

Near at hand the tone of the water-drum is often a dull thud, but when properly tuned by an experienced drummer it has a resonance and peculiarly pleasing quality, even at close range. However, one has but to depart some distance from the drum to be convinced that there is volume in the water-drum undreamed of when near to it, and the enchantment of its voice increases with the distance. No drum can be heard so far—it is on record that water-drums have been heard eight to ten miles over a lake. This capacity to be heard distinctly at a distance, coupled with a peculiar tone quality and a temperamental nature, gives to the water-drum an intrigue that makes it beloved by all who know it.

There are two types of water-drums, those made of pottery and those of a hollow log with a solid waterproof bottom. The earthen-pot drums were common among many eastern and southern tribes in the ancient days, those of the South using a semicircular-shaped bowl with legs as shown in the accompanying drawing (Figure 77). The pottery water-drum of the Pueblo Indians, much used today, is a vase-shaped pot with a flared out top as shown in Figure 78. These are filled about one-fourth full of water and the wet hide tied over the top.

The hollow-log drum of the Woodland Indians which will be described in detail presently is the more common type.

The woods-dwelling tribes made far greater use of water-drums than any other Indians, and attached a greater significance to them. To the Chippewas and their many neighboring tribes of the north-central areas, for example, the water-drum is a true medicine drum of unusual potency, the sacred drum of the Medicine Society or Mide (Midewin or Midewiwin), which society constitutes one of the chief phases of Chippewa religion. Reserved for the sacred ceremonies of the Midewin

Fig. 77—*Water-drum typical of the Southern Tribes.*

Fig. 78—*Earthen Water-drum from the Southwest Indians.*

(Grand Medicine) the water-drum is seldom seen or heard by the casual visitor among these Indians. The old Chippewas I have known, who are reluctant to discuss their medicine drums, have after years of friendship disclosed many secrets of the dream-dance drum and the medicine hoop-drums, but remain tight-lipped and non-committal regarding the water-drums, and needless to say, have refused to make them for other than their own use.

Let us first describe how to make authentic Indian water-drums and then take up the use of modern materials in fashioning these drums.

THE LOG WATER-DRUM OF THE
WOODLAND INDIANS

Secure a hollow basswood or cedar log which, when the bark is removed and the outside smoothed up, is about twelve inches in diameter. The Indians would burn and dig out the center if a hollow one could not be found. Cut off a sixteen- or seventeen-inch section of this and hollow it out with a chisel or mallet just as in making the log tombés described on page 120, bringing it down to a thin shell. The drum is slightly smaller at the top than at the bottom: Granted that the log is of the same diameter throughout, taper it slightly toward the top end by shaving off the outside with a drawknife so that its top diameter is about an inch less than the bottom. Since the inside diameter is the same throughout, this tapering produces a shell the rim of which is thinner at the top than at the bottom. The thickness of the rim may be an inch and a quarter at the bottom but should be no more than a half to three-fourths of an inch at the top.

Now a circular disc of basswood or cedar must be cut out and fitted into the bottom, this disc being one inch thick. The disc is forced up into the hollow log so that it is about a half inch from the bottom and consequently the log should be made a trifle thinner for a distance of an inch and a half from the bottom to accommodate the disc when it is installed. To make the disc, place the hollow log on the basswood or cedar board and run a pencil line around the inside edge thus marking the circumference on the board. Saw out the circular piece roughly outside this line and then whittle it down with a knife until it fits very snugly into the bottom of the drumframe. The bottom is then made watertight by the use of pine-pitch into which a little powdered charcoal or lampblack is mixed. Having smeared the edges of the disc with this black mixture and forced it into place in the bottom of the hollow log, fill the crack around the outside of the bottom with a thick layer of pitch. The bottom is completed by splitting in half a black ash or maple sapling, one inch in diameter, and bending it around the outside as shown in Figure 79. The sapling is held in place by thongs of rawhide binding the ends together where they overlap; to accomplish this, the rawhide thongs are loosely wrapped around the overlapping ends, then the bent sapling is forced tightly together around the hollow log and held while someone tightens the rawhide thongs and ties them securely.

Now a bunghole of about an inch and a half in diameter must be bored through the side a little over half of the way up, as shown in Figure 79, and a stick whittled to serve as a bung, this stick being long enough to extend out the width of the hand.

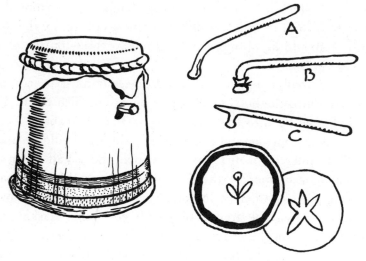

Fig. 79—*Woodland Indian Water-drums.*

In contrast to other types of drums, the water-drum head is of heavy buckskin (tanned hide) rather than rawhide, although the latter can be used with good results. The drumhead should be rectangular in shape so as to hang down at the corners as shown in Figure 79. The hide is not laced as in other drums, but is put on temporarily each time the drum is used and held in place by a hoop forced over it as shown in Figure 79. Whittle the hoop out of white cedar and bend as directed for making the hand-drum hoops on page 38. It should be large enough to fit loosely over the head of the drum. Now wrap it with several layers of stripped cloth until it is large enough so as to fit very snugly over the top of the log when the drumhead is in place.

Fig. 80—*Cross-section of a Chippewa Water-drum.*

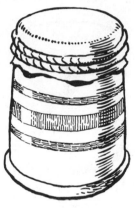

Fig. 81
A Menominee Water-drum.

Fill the drum about a quarter full of water as illustrated in the drawing of the cross-section in Figure 80. Soak the drumhead well and put in place. This completes the drum and it is now ready to use. When not in use it should be emptied and the drumhead rolled up and placed inside.

Tuning the Drum.—Water-drums are used with a wet drumhead. With the drum about one-fourth full of water and the wet hide in place, beat it and if the tone is flat and dull, dry the head a little by the fire and try it out again. Continue this process until the drum develops the satisfactory tone. The

Chippewa drummers tune their drums at great length by drying the head, shaking the drum so as to splash more water on
it, and thus experimenting until it booms to their satisfaction.

One will have to experiment at some length with a water-
drum to ascertain just how the best results may be obtained.
Try out the drumhead at various degrees of dryness and then
if good results are not obtained, experiment with the amount
of water in the drum, using the bunghole to change the water
level.

Decorating the Water-Drum.—The log water-drums of the

Fig. 82
Chippewa Water-drum.

Fig. 83
Potawatomi Water-drums.

woods Indians have very little decoration—sometimes none.
The outside of the log is usually plain, or if decorated has nothing more than a few stripes of color. These stripes may be in
red, blue, and yellow around the bottom of the log as in the
Chippewa drum shown in Figure 79, or in red and blue around
the middle as shown in the Menominee drum in Figure 81. It
will be noted that this Menominee drum has two hoops, one
above the other. Occassionally one sees a Chippewa drum with
slanting upright lines as on that shown in Figure 82, these
lines being in black. A more highly ornamented drum from the

Potawatomis is shown in Figure 83: the drumhead is in red with a black spot in the middle and a black line around the edge; the rawhide extending down the sides has a red line around it near the top, below which it is solid black. There is a black and a blue line around the log at the bottom.

Occasionally a water-drum will have a simple decoration on the inside and outside of the bottom. Figure 79 shows bottom designs from a Minnesota Chippewa water-drum.

Water-Drum Thumpers.—A water-drum thumper is of a different type than those used for any other kind of drum. It is usually a curved stick about three-eighths of an inch in diameter, shaped as in A and B, Figure 79, the drum being struck with the end only. These are made out of hardwood, usually oak, and are from nine to twelve inches long. Another type, clearly illustrated in C, Figure 79, has a two-inch projection at right angles to the main stick. All of these beaters have a knob on the end very slightly larger than the rest of the stick. Sometimes this knob is covered with a layer of buckskin, but more frequently the wood is brought in contact with the drumhead without a covering.

PUEBLO WATER-DRUMS

The Pueblo earthern water-drums vary in size from small pots holding a gallon of water up to huge ones measuring thirty or more inches in diameter. They are of the general shape of that shown in Figure 84, this drawing being made from a Pueblo drum seven inches high, six inches in diameter and holding a gallon and a half. These drums are of dark undecorated pottery and are rigged up into a drum for the occasion and not kept. Any bowl-shaped piece of pottery so designed that a drumhead can be tied to its top would be usable.

When not in use the tanned drumhead and rawhide thong for tying it are kept inside the pot. To prepare for use, fill the pot about one-fourth full of water, soak the hide well, stretch it tightly over the top and fasten by wrapping the rawhide thong around the narrow neck and tying. Allow the hide to dry a little and try out the drum; if it is too high pitched splash a little of the inside water on the drumhead and try again, thus experimenting until the best tone is produced. When being used the drum should be held off the ground by grasping the edge of the rawhide below the thong.

Fig. 84—*Southwest Indian Water-drum.*

Pottery Water-drum Thumpers. — The thumper used on pottery drums is shown in Figure 84. It is about twelve inches long when finished—a stick thinned down at the end, the thinned part bent into a circle, and lashed. The drum is struck with the curved part.

WATER-DRUMS OF MODERN MATERIALS

Drumframes.—No better water-drum could be asked for than a five-gallon *keg*. Used ones can frequently be picked up at grocery stores or new ones purchased in any city or from mail-order houses. Merely remove the top, and replace the short bung with a stick whittled to fit the hole, long enough to be grasped with the hand and easily withdrawn. Make the hoop with which to hold the drumhead from cheese-box wood. It should be about one and one-fourth inches wide and large enough to slip loosely over the top of the keg. Wrap it with several layers of stripped cloth until it fits very snugly over the top of the keg. Either rawhide or buckskin (or any piece of thin leather like buckskin) may be used for the drumhead. After the keg is filled one-fourth full of water, place this hide over the top and then force the hoop in place as shown in

Figure 85. The drum is tuned and played in the same way as the log water-drum already described.

A small hand water-drum may be made from a one-gallon keg.

A gallon tin can of heavy tin such as cookies frequently are packed in will make a good water-drum. Fill one-fourth full of water and tie the hide around the sides near the top.

A temporary water-drum may be rigged up by merely tying the drumhead over the top of a galvanized bucket, granite kettle or any similar container. When the dancing is over, the drumhead may be removed and the utensil returned to its original duty in the kitchen.

Drumheads.—Split rawhide drumheads can usually be obtained from music stores that will do good service on water-drums,

Fig. 85—*Water-drum made from a keg.*

requiring only a small-size piece as they do. Buckskin can usually be obtained easily, and if not, chamois makes a fair substitute.

Interesting experiments may be made with cloth for water-drum heads. Canvas and heavy linen will *shrink when they are wet*—in this respect acting in the opposite fashion from rawhide. If the water-drum is covered with one of these materials tacked around the edge it will give only a dull thump; but when thoroughly wet by splashing water from within the drum on it, and rubbing water into it from the top, it will tighten up and give a delightful tone. Experimentation will determine the proper degree of wetness.

Drumsticks

CERTAIN kinds of Indian drums call for certain types of drumsticks, due in part to the demands of tradition but more largely because experience has shown that certain styles of thumpers seem to fit some drums better than others, and serve better to bring out the tone qualities. There are hard beaters, semi-hard beaters, and soft beaters; long beaters and short beaters; straight beaters, curved beaters, and beaters with a circular crook on the drum end. Some are considered appropriate for one style of drum, some for another; some are preferred by one tribe, some by other tribes.

The Indian prized his drumstick, indeed often considering it as important as the drum itself. And when it comes to a sacred medicine drum, the thumper becomes a consideration of grave importance, because the wrong style of thumper might nullify the spirit power normally within the drum. Such drums usually have beaters that are kept with them constantly and used for no other purpose.

Let us consider the various types of beaters and the use to which each can be put, but first the important question of the kind of wood for thumpers must be discussed.

WOOD FOR DRUMSTICKS

Drumsticks should be made of strong *hardwood*. The best beaters are long and very slender, so slender that they give and spring when struck against the drum. Soft and brittle wood will break if made thin enough for a good thumper, and furthermore does not have the necessary weight. The best wood is *white oak*—so say the woods-dwelling Indians who know well the qualities of woods and who live where an abundance of varieties exist from which to choose. No other wood will be used by them if white oak is obtainable. If oak cannot be had the following are acceptable: hickory, ironwood, ash, elm.

Never use a branch of one of these trees for a drumstick, but rather a section cut out of the trunk of a young sapling and whittled down to dimensions—trunk wood is much stronger. *Select a sapling of white oak or one of the other woods two inches in diameter*—the wood from such a sapling will be stronger by far and much more pliable than will that supplied by a limb of equal thickness cut from a large tree. A two-foot section from such a sapling will furnish wood for eight excellent drumsticks.

Here, then, are the two rules for the selection of drumstick wood: (1) use strong, pliable hardwood, (2) cut the wood from the trunk of a sapling, not from a branch of a large tree.

If you must use materials to be found in cities, three-eighths inch dowling will serve reasonably well.

HARD DRUMSTICKS

For all hand-drums (Chapter III) and the large dance-drums (Chapter IV):

Long, slender hard beaters are the favorites of the Woodland Indians and are without equal for use on hand-drums and dance-drums of the tub type. Such drums are much less effective if used with a softened beater, the hard beater producing the sharp, clear, definite boom and precise rhythm that is an aid to dancing always. The Chippewas prefer these long, slender, straight beaters with little or no padding for every-day use on dance and hand-drums, but for ceremonial use and on sacred medicine drums such as the dream-dance drum and the medicine-rattle hand-drums, use the hard beaters with circular ends described in the section following.

From a two-inch sapling of white oak or other hardwood cut off a two-foot length that is round, smooth, and free from knots. Split this lengthwise into eighths as indicated in A, Figure 86. Select one of the eighths and whittle it down into a round stick one-half inch in thickness. This accomplished, thin down the middle section of the stick still more for a distance of six inches, bringing it down to three-eighths inch or slightly less. We thus have a stick one-half inch wide for a distance of about eight inches at each end and gradually thinned down at the middle to three-eighths inch, as shown in C, Figure 86. Round off the ends and remove all sharp edges. The narrower section at the middle gives the drumstick a slight whip when it is used vigorously on a big dance-drum.

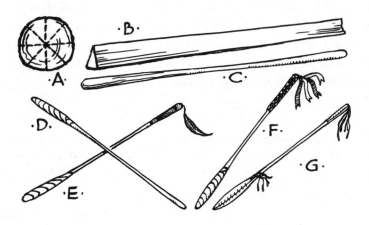

Fig. 86—*Hard drumsticks.*

We now have a hard beater that can be considered finished as it stands, although it is usually customary to wrap the drum end with a thin layer of cloth. Tear up some colored cloth into strips one-inch wide and wrap these around one end as shown in D, Figure 86, the wrapped area covering about seven inches. This wrapped end should not be over three-fourths inches thick at the most, since we want a *hard* and not a padded drumstick. With the wrapping in place and the ends tied tightly, it is well to sew the edges of the cloth strips to prevent them from working loose.

In G, Figure 86 we have a thumper that has a thin wrapping of cloth on the end over which a covering of buckskin has been sewed, the whole being three-fourths of an inch thick. On the hand end there is also a covering of buckskin with a tassel of buckskin strips.

Beaters of this type usually do not have much ornamentation. Colored cloth is often selected for the wrapping and sometimes there is added handle decorations as in E and F, Figure 86. In E there are painted stripes for a distance of about six inches from the end, whereas in F, the end is wrapped with ribbon of two colors, the ribbon being allowed to hang down for a distance of six or eight inches. Occasionally the entire stick is wrapped with colored cloth.

How to Use Hard Beaters.—A hard drumstick of this type is struck sidewise against the drumhead. A beater with a large padded knob on the end would be handled so as to strike the drum with the padded end only, but not so with these hard beaters—they are held parallel to the drumhead and slapped against it. This being the case a long stick is needed—thus the twenty-four inch length.

DRUMSTICKS WITH CURVED ENDS

For medicine hand-drums and dance-drums:

Here is a fancy and very effective hard drumstick for use on the more elaborate hand-drums and dance-drums, the straight beaters described in the preceding section being for every-day use on ordinary drums. Figure 87 shows the curved type so popular among the Chippewas and neighboring woodland tribes. This drumstick has much rebound and resiliency when the circular part is struck against the drum as indicated in Figure 89.

The finished drumstick is twenty inches long, seven-sixteenths to one-half inch thick, with the circular end measuring three inches in diameter. To make it a thirty-inch piece if oak or ash is needed, cut from a sapling as described for hard drumsticks in the preceding section. The twenty-inch section that is to be the handle should be whittled into a smooth, round stick seven-sixteenths to one-half inch thick. The remaining ten inches should be thinned down into a flat piece of the same width but only one-eighth inch thick, as shown in A, Figure

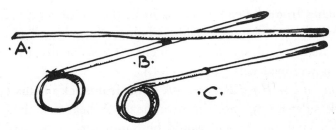

Fig. 87—*Curved drumsticks.*

87. Submerge the stick in water for a few hours and then bend the thin end into the three-inch circle shown in B, and lash the end to the main stick with a wet rawhide thong. A piece of wet rawhide is usually wrapped around that part of the stick that is curved, and sewed as shown in C, but if the wood is carefully smoothed off so that there are no sharp edges, it may be used without covering.

The drummers sitting around the big dance-drum in the round dance-house of the Chippewas are pretty sure to be equipped with these beaters with circular ends. If it is a dream-dance or a similarly ornamented drum (Chapter IV) or a highly decorated hand-drum with medicine rattles (Chapter

III), the drumsticks will probably be much ornamented; usually with beaver fur. Figure 88 shows such a drumstick with beaver fur—the beaver hide is an untanned one, cut up into strips, wrapped around the stick, and sewed. There is a

Fig. 88—*A Chippewa ceremonial drumstick.*

tuft of ribbons at the center and a tassel of one-inch colored ribbons at the end. This is a rich, beautiful drumstick—beaver fur will add dignity and richness to any object and is beloved on drumsticks by the Woodland Indians. So decorated, we have a true medicine drumstick. In case beaver fur cannot be had, any fur may be substituted, or instead of fur, colored ribbons used as wrappings throughout the length of the stick.

Remember that sticks with curved ends are handled by striking the curved side against the drum—that is, the edge away from the handle, as indicated in Figure 89.

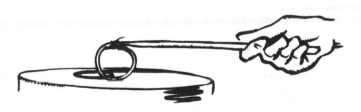

Fig. 89—*How to use the curved drumstick.*

RATTLE DRUMSTICKS

For Medicine hand-drums and dance-drums:

Instead of the curved drumsticks just described, rattle beaters are sometimes used on medicine drums, made by covering the circular end of the curved stick with rawhide, thus turning it into a tiny drum, inside of which a handful of small pebbles is placed (Figure 90). The rattle from these pebbles can be heard distinctly when the drumstick is used on a dance-drum and the effect is most pleasing and interesting.

The stick for the rattle beater is made exactly as for the curved beater described in the preceding section, except that the circular end should be a trifle larger—three and one-half inches to four inches in diameter. The circular end is covered with rawhide and sewed at the edges just as in making a hand-drum—the details of construction are set forth in Chapter IX, "Dance-rattles," under the heading, "Drumstick Rattles."

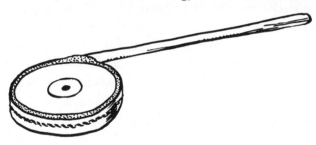

Fig. 90—*A rattle drumstick.*

SEMI-HARD DRUMSTICKS

For single-headed hand-drums:

The Plains Indians usually pad their beaters a little more than their woodland brothers, thus making them a little softer. These are made in exactly the same way as the hard beaters described earlier in this chapter except that the wrapping of cloth strips on the end is thicker, perhaps an inch or an inch and one-eighth, and is not extended as far from the end, usually not over four inches. This cloth wrapping may be left as it is or covered with buckskin. Occasionally the cloth is wrapped over the entire length of the stick, there being but one layer over the main area beyond the padded end.

Fig. 91—A semi-hard drumstick.

Figure 91 shows a Sioux beater of this type with the padding made of cloth strips covered with tanned hide. The padded end is one and one-fourth inches wide and one inch thick, thus producing two broad surfaces that are used for striking the drums, the narrow sides being covered with beading.

Among the Indians of Alaska and the Northwest 'Coast a shorter, stockier beater is seen with a semi-hard padded knob on the end, this same type occasionally appearing among thc Plains Indians. The stick is about twelve inches long and three-quarters inch thick. There is a slight knob of wood at the end to prevent the padding from slipping, over which cloth strips are wrapped and a covering of skin tied.

SOFT BEATERS

For Southwest Tombés:

The hollow-log drums of the Southwest call for a softer beater such as that shown in Figure 92. The stick should be eighteen inches long and three-eighths to one-half inch thick, with a slightly wider knob on the end to prevent the padded head from slipping off. The Pueblo Indian would pad the end with down from the eagle, then cover it with tanned hide tied firmly to the stick. Cotton is a good substitute for eagle down. The

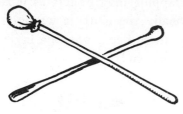

padded ball should be about one and one-half inches in diameter.

These soft beaters are not recommended for other kinds of drums than those of the Southwest hollow-log type (Chapter V).

Fig. 92—*A soft drumstick.*

WATER-DRUM BEATERS

The special types of drumsticks required for water-drums are described in Chapter VI, "Water-Drums."

Using the Primitive Drum

DRUMS of the primitive type described in these chapters require a different type of care, are tuned in a different way, and are beaten to produce a different type of rhythm, than is the case with modern band and orchestra drums. This chapter will discuss the care and use of the primitive drums described throughout the pages of the book.

TESTING THE NEW DRUM

No two hand-made tomtoms are just alike and one cannot know what quality of instrument he has created until it has thoroughly dried and been tested—this is one of the chief fascinations of drum-making and one of the reasons why a person is moved to make more and more drums, knowing that each will have a temperament and tone quality all its own.

A little experimentation in beating a new drum will probably indicate that the sound varies depending on where the drumstick is applied—one spot may give one tone, another spot, another; it is often possible to produce three or four different sounds on a single drumhead. Furthermore there may be a dead spot that gives forth nothing more than a dull thump. Then, too, if it is a two-headed drum, the two heads may differ so much in tone quality as to sound like two different drums. These facts being true, it is necessary to experiment with the drum until just the right spot is discovered where the best sound can be produced, and conversely, the areas that should be avoided.

Moreover, the tone of the drum will change with the tightness of the heads. In its normal degree of tightness it may be too high-pitched and "tin-panny," or perhaps too loose and rumbly. We must test it out to determine just the right tension for the most pleasing results, and then tune it to that degree each time, following the tuning instructions in the section following.

Some drums must be struck with force if they are to give their best performance, others must be tapped gently, and here again experimentation is necessary. If mere noise is all that is wanted, the drummer can lay to with all his force, the harder the better, but the resulting clatter may be a grave injustice to a delicate tomtom capable of pleasing quality if properly handled. And right here it should be said that most beginners hammer their drums much too vigorously, the ruinous force straining the drum and achieving nothing but harshness. A good drum does not need to be beaten severely. Each tomtom has its own vibration point at which the boom will be most pleasing and far-carrying—to force it beyond this point is distressing to the listener and ruinous to the drum.

TUNING THE DRUM

A drumhead becomes loose and slack, and therefore dull and flat in tone, when it is damp or cold, and conversely, it becomes tight and higher pitched when hot. A band drum has mechanical tightening and loosening attachments by which it can be quickly tuned regardless of dampness and temperature, but not so in the case of the primitive drums with which we are interested, the only way to tune these being to change the temperature.

If the drum is too loose, its boom lacking or deadened, its tone dull, its reverberations nil, as is so often the case with these hand-made drums particularly on damp days and in the evening, all that needs to be done is to hold it next to the fire for a few moments—it will gradually tighten up, and by thumping it every few seconds the desirable degree of tightness can be determined. Similarly, if it is too tight to sound well, it can be loosened by cooling it, or if necessary, by dampening it.

The heating process must be done slowly and carefully—to allow it to become too hot will probably split the drumhead or if not will stretch it so much that it will become looser than ever at ordinary temperatures; to place it so close to the fire that it becomes burnt before it has time to tighten will render it permanently flat and lifeless.

The average laced drum, if the hide were stretched to the proper tightness in making it, will produce the proper sound at ordinary living temperature, becoming too loose only at times when there is much moisture in the air, and too tight at times of extreme heat—consequently tuning does not often become an annoying problem.

An Indian kneeling before a fire in front of the round dance-house, carefully warming the big dance-drum, is a common sight just before the dancing is to start. Should it be a damp evening, the fire is kept going throughout the dance so that the drum can be tightened at frequent intervals. Often on such damp days, two drums are employed, one being warmed while the other is in use.

Drums with canvas drumheads are tuned by reversing the procedure used for rawhide heads, that is, the drumhead is made tight by wetting it. Water must be poured over the canvas and rubbed in with the hands so that the cloth becomes soaked all the way through. This will take some little time since canvas is made to resist water. Once soaked, the canvas tightens so as to give forth a pleasant sound.

The tuning of water-drums is discussed in Chapter VI, "Water-Drums."

CARING FOR THE DRUMS

Drums should be kept away from moisture as much as possible. They should never be taken out into the rain unless well covered; although they will tighten again in drying, yet actual contact of water on the drumhead is always detrimental to it. Furthermore, the drum should be kept away from extreme heat and cold, and should be protected from frequent changes in temperature since the constant tightening and loosening that such changes cause will wear the drum out more quickly than constant drumming on it would do. The drum is at its best in the normal living temperature of a house where wide fluctuations of course seldom occur. Therefore, the best place for it is hanging on the wall of your home—there is then no danger of anything falling on it and breaking the thin drumhead, nor of sudden changes of temperature doing it harm. Do not hang it above a register or radiator, however, or you will probably take it down some day to find the drumhead split from the heat —many a drum has been ruined in this way; there is of course more heat near the ceiling than near the floor, and the ceiling is hotter over a register than one might think.

SIMPLE INDIAN DRUM RHYTHMS

The rhythms used in Indian dances, songs, and ceremonials are frequently intricate, diverse, and involve frequent changes. Singing almost always accompanies the dance, and the drumming follows the song. A study of any of the books recording Indian music will indicate the variety of rhythms, and the drumming can be worked out from the recorded music.[1]

---

[1] Consult such books as the following:
> Besse Evans and Mary E. Evans: *American Indian Dance Steps.* New York: A. S. Barnes and Company, 1931.
> Julia Buttree: *The Rhythm of the Redman.* New York: A. S. Barnes and Company, 1930.
> Natalie Curtis: *The Indians' Book.* New York: Harper and Brothers, 1907.

For the purpose of this book an indication of the more common simple dance drumming of the Indians is all that is necessary. Usually there are two drumbeats to each quarter note of the music, that is the dancing is accompanied by drumbeats in eighth notes.

The most common drumming consists of beats in groups of two, the first beat accented: *loud,* soft; *loud,* soft, etc. It aids the drummer to count to himself as he beats: *One* and, *two* and, etc.

Again we very frequently find a steady unaccented beat, to which the drummer would count, *one, two, three, four,* etc.

Less frequently we find the drumbeats in groups of four with the first one accented: *Loud,* soft, soft, soft. The count for this would be, *one,* two, three, four, *one,* two, three, four, etc. Similarly, but still more rarely, beats are in groups of three with the first accented: *loud,* soft, soft; with the count, *one,* two, three.

In all of these rhythms, the drumstick is allowed to rebound freely from the drumhead. There is a type of drumming, however, in which every other beat is made by holding the stick against the drumhead as long as possible, removing it just in time to dispatch the stroke for the next beat.

This is characteristic of the rhythm of the Chippewa wardance. The beats are in groups of two, the second one accented. The first and unaccented beat is made by allowing the stick to rebound, and the second and accented one, by holding it against the drumhead. The count is: and *one,* and *two,* etc.

PLAYING THE LARGE DANCE-DRUM

The large dance-drums described in Chapter IV are usually "played" by a group of from four to eight drummers seated in a circle around it and plying their beaters against it in unison. As the Indians would do it, the drummers take turns in singing, the one who sings setting the rhythm of the drumming for the others who fall in and follow after the song has started.

Suspend the drums from poles as described in Chapter IV and seat or stand the group of drummers around it, each equipped with one of the long, slender, hard drumsticks described in Chapter VII. Without a song to serve as a guide, inexperienced drummers frequently have trouble in getting together and staying together with the beating. While practice will relieve this, it will always be necessary to have one serve as director and set the rhythm. This director should beat alone for about eight beats whereupon the remainder, having thus obtained the count, join in. In similar fashion the director indicates the strength of the beating, raising his arm high for the loud sections and lowering it for the soft drumming.

The drumsticks are normally raised high with each beat, usually perpendicular to the ground, and whipped down sharply.

RHYTHM BANDS

The radiant joy on the faces of children in rhythm bands in schools, clubs, and camps is proof sufficient of the appeal of rhythm and drumming. These drum-and-rattle bands seem to awaken an elemental sort of joy in both children and adults, and are unexcelled as a source of entertainment to the participants even though the listeners may not always appreciate the resultant noise. At the same time, these orchestras serve admirably as education in rhythm. Tomtom bands are scarcely characteristic of the Indians, although the Plains Indian dancing frequently is accompanied by several drummers each with a hand-drum rather than one big dance-drum; hand-drums that harmonize together are selected for this purpose.

If our rhythm orchestra is to be kept under control there should be a large central drum to set the rhythm and serve somewhat the same purpose as the bass-drum in the band—one of the large dance-drums described in Chapter IV is ideal for this. Group the other types of drums together around the central drum, the hand-drums in one place, the log-drums in another, etc. Then group the rattles described in Chapter IX together, likewise the *moraches* and the bull-roarers. Dancing bells may also be used, these being tied around the ankles and sounded by jarring the heels against the floor.

Under the baton of the director, and following the lead of the big dance-drum handled by an experienced drummer, the whole group "make music" together.

THE USE OF INDIAN DRUMS TODAY

Let us now consider the use that can be made of the Indian drums described in these chapters by the various educational-recreational agencies today.

Drums in Organized Camps

Most organized camps feel that the ideal camp craft is one that relies on woodsy materials and is associated with primitive life, and further, that the value of the craft is increased if it produces objects that are useful *in camp* and not merely gadgets to take home and show mother. On all of these points Indian drum-making registers as having few equals. The craft involves the fashioning of a frame of wood—perhaps chopping, whittling and bending a cedar board into a hoop—and the handling and applying of rawhide. The techniques are strictly primitive and, moreover, are drawn from the most successful and gifted of all woodsmen and campers—the American Indians. *And the finished product has many uses in camp*. What are these uses?

Drums offer a picturesque substitute for the bugle as a camp call. One of the large dance-drums centrally located in a hanger will boom forth its message to the far corners of the campsite, calling the campers to meals and to activities. Singing the Zuni Sunrise Song as he plays, the drummer awakens the campers in the morning with an appropriate touch of beauty, and in similar fashion puts them to sleep at night in the way of the woods with the Zuni Sunset Song. Some camps employ several types of calls in the course of the day, using the drum at such times as it seems particularly appropriate.

When the campers have gathered in the dining hall a stroke of the hand-drum pleasantly asks for silence preliminary to the saying of grace. At the end of the meal it again requests attention to the announcements, and finally gives the signal for departure. The drum performs this duty much more pleasingly and fits the situation more appropriately than the customary whistle.

How could a council fire or council-ring ceremony be appropriately conducted without a drum? The council ring itself is Indian and the ceremony at least has elements of Indian tradition in it—obviously something vital would be missing if there were no Indian drum. The drum provided the dance beat of the Indian's dance-drama, the pulse beat of the throbbing life-drama of the Redman's council fire—it is equally the beat of the modern council ring.

Drums are a requisite to dancing in organized camps today, whether it be Indian dancing, interpretative dancing of the ballet type, or any form of modern rhythmic interpretation. Yes, drums are essential, and Indian drums best fit the American camp picture. With true camp spirit, they should be made, not bought.

As a starting signal for races and athletic events, a sharp stroke of a drum serves the purpose quite as well as does a starter's gun, and is more in keeping with the spirit of camping.

Lastly, drums are good playthings in camp—campers love to

beat them. Rhythm bands are always joyous camp features. Whether used alone or with others, drums furnish a happy and deeply satisfying means of expression.

Drums—many of them—belong in camp.

Drums in Dancing Groups

Drums have been associated with dancing since the beginning of time, and even in the modern world with its perfection of the many instruments comprising the symphony orchestra, there is a very definite trend back toward the use of simple percussion instruments alone for many of the modern dance forms. It is obvious on the face of it that drums are essential to the rhythm of dancing. And if percussion alone is to be used, there are no drums that seem so completely appropriate and satisfying to the dance as primitive tomtoms.

For everyday use in dancing instruction in studios and in physical education departments, the Indian hand-drum is ideal —light, convenient, and possessing a strong, pleasing tone. For the handling of large groups of dancers, the big dance-drum offers strength and volume, together with the sharp, distinct rhythm essential to such dancing situations. For stage recitals, primitive drums possess a decorative quality that never fails to intrigue.

An assortment of the various types of drums set forth in these chapters seems indispensable in any dancing group or class. Such an array will offer the opportunity to select the drum that seems best to fit the dance in question.

Lastly, the craft of drum-making can be integrated with dancing instruction with most satisfactory results.

Drums in the Gymnasium

Primitive drums seem to belong in the gymnasium—of all the rhythm instruments they possess an elemental quality that somehow symbolizes big-muscle activity. If dancing is a part of the gym program, drums are of course indispensable. They likewise provide rhythm for marching and other physical movements. Even if a piano or victrola is available, there are many situations when a drum is definitely preferable.

A drum makes a good starting signal for every-day use in a gym, being less expensive to operate during practice periods than a starter's gun and causes less in the way of an annoying explosion. They serve well as gongs to attract attention and to secure silence in the gym. There are many who seek to reduce the use of the whistle to the minimum and find a colorful substitute in a drum.

Many unexpected uses will be found for a handy-sized Indian drum—every gymnasium should possess one.

Drums on the Playground

The perennial appeal of drums to children make them the best of adjuncts on a playground. They add momentum and zest to singing games and children's dances. They serve as a signal or call for changing activities or the announcing of time. They make possible rhythm bands. As in the gymnasium, they may be used as a substitute for a starter's gun in racing events. Withal, if of the primitive type, they carry a strong imaginative appeal. They are good and useful things to have on the children's playground.

Drumcraft using such objects as tin cans and cardboard cartons for frames is an excellent and inexpensive addition to the playground craft program.

Drums in Boys' and Girls' Clubs

Any club for boys and girls that builds its program on primitive-lore, pioneer crafts, or camping will find in primitive drums an unusual appeal. In their every aspect they fit such a situation. From the standpoint of utility they offer all the values listed for organized camps and gymnasiums in connection with crafts, dancing, rhythm, signals, etc., and when not in use they make ideal wall hangings for the clubroom.

Drums in Music Classes

Many are the creative music classes in schools across the country that feature the fashioning of drums of the primitive pattern, and find in it an indispensable tool, much loved by children and of great value educationally. What could be of more educational significance in such groups than bringing out through actual crafts how primitive man used his intelligence to create musical instruments from the materials he found available? Children's music classes in schools find much use for drums in singing games, rhythmic play, and training in rhythm.

Dance Rattles and Other
Sound-Makers

RATTLES are almost as indispensable to dancing in the eyes of most Indian tribes as is the drum. They are as universal among the Indians as are drums and usually hold a place of prestige almost equal to that of the drum. Not all dances call for rattles but some rituals could not be performed without them; in fact, some use no drums at all, the only sound being the clicking of the rattles in the hands of the dancers.

Sometimes the use of the rattles is confined to drummers, some of whom beat the drums and others shake the rattles. Again, and more frequently, the dancers themselves handle the rattles, each carrying one in his hand and shaking it as he steps. Used in this way the rattle is an inspiration to the dancer, its rattling sound serving as a constant incentive to perform, and moreover, it serves as an aid to rhythmic movement—it seems to make possible the achievement of all movements in harmony with the rhythm with less effort. And needless to say the rhythmic clicking of the rattles adds a marked element of interest to the dance from the spectators' point of view. All this in addition to the medicine power the rattle is supposed to possess and its potency in accomplishing the purpose of the dance!

As we shall see presently, Indian rattles are of many types and made out of many kinds of materials. Those of the hollow-shell type have loose objects within that are shaken against the sides to produce the sound. These objects may be small pebbles or buckshot, depending on the nature of the sound desired, but in addition *there must be seeds of some sort:* Gourd rattles of the Southwest contain the gourd seeds; Chippewa rattles regardless of type usually have kernels of corn or grains of wild rice within; the Cherokee and other Southern tribes put grains of Indian wheat inside; often one finds rattles containing dried peas in addition to the pebbles. Seeds are considered necessary if the rattle is to have potency.

This chapter will consider not only rattles but *moraches* or *guayos, bullroarers, dancing bells* and *tinkles*. All of these sound-makers are valuable in many types of dancing today, and all are excellent for recreational use.

DANCE-RATTLES

Dance-rattles are of two general types, those that consist of a hollow shell with rattle devices within, and those that have the rattle devices attached to a stick or other object. The hollow-shell rattles are as follows, each of which will be discussed in turn: *gourd rattles, drumstick rattles, rawhide rattles, steer-horn rattles, birch-bark rattles, turtle-shell rattles, wooden rattles, sea-shell rattles, tin-can rattles,* and *cocoanut rattles.*

Those with the rattle devices attached to a stick or other object are as follows: *turtle-shell leg rattles,* and *hoof, bone, and tin-tinkle rattles.*

Gourd Rattles

Of all of the types of rattles, those made from gourds are the most widely used among the various Indian tribes—they are prominent in the culture of the Indians of the Southwest, Plains, Northern and Eastern Woodlands, Southern, and California areas. And of all the rattles, none are easier to make or more interesting as a simple craft.

A dried gourd will serve as a rattle just as it is—the neck serves as a convenient handle and the seeds within strike against the dried sides with a rattle sound when it is shaken. However, the sound produced is soft and muffled as compared to that obtainable after the inside is cleaned out and pebbles added.

Gourds of any size and shape may be used for rattles, varying from little round ones two inches in diameter up to those a foot across. The average gourd rattle measures four to six inches in diameter and gourds of this size are in greatest demand among the Indians. These should be secured if possible and allowed to dry out thoroughly.

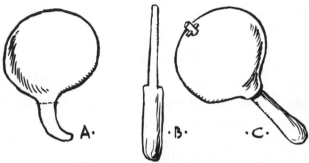

Fig. 93—*Construction of Gourd Rattles.*

Among the Southwest Indians, particularly the Pueblos and Hopis, gourd rattles are used in dancing today in the same way they have been for countless years and are still regarded by the Indians as possessing the same strong medicine that their ancestors attributed to them. Happily these Southwest peoples have resisted to a remarkable degree the inroads of so-called western culture.

How to Make a Gourd Rattle.—The gourd rattles of the Pueblos and Hopis are of two main types. Let us consider making the simplest of these first—that shown in Figure 93. Secure a dry gourd about five inches in diameter of the shape shown in A, saw off the neck with an ordinary saw close to the globe and then bore a three-eighth inch hole in the blossom end (directly opposite the neck) with the point of an ordinary jackknife blade. Shake out the seeds and all loose debris and then run a heavy wire through the hole and scrape the sides with it, working loose as much of the dry pulp as possible. Since it gives the rattle a muffled sound if left in, it will pay to take plenty of time to scrape out the pith thoroughly. Now a stick of soft wood must be whittled to the shape shown in B, just large enough to slip through the two holes, with a shoulder as indicated against which the neck end of the gourd is to rest. The handle part of the stick should be about five inches long. Care should be taken to prepare a stick that fits very snugly. Put a small handful of tiny pebbles into the gourd (large ones do not produce a good sound) and then put back into it a dozen of the gourd seeds which were removed—remember that the seeds are necessary to give the rattle potency as medicine. (The Chippewa put kernels of corn in their gourd rattles, and the Cherokee and other Southern tribes add grains of Indian wheat.) Insert the stick as shown in C, and secure by boring a small hole at the blossom end, through which a little peg of wood should be forced as indicated in C. Present-day Indians sometimes wrap a string around the stick next to the blossom end, thus creating a ridge that supports the gourd, but the peg is the traditional and preferred method.

The rattle is now completed and ready for decoration, and here, as in drum ornamentation, the design should be an authentic Indian one in every detail. The Southwest Indians give grave concern to the details of the gourd designs since they are used in religious dances. Water-coloring should be used on the gourds—showcard paint, caked water-colors, or powder mixed with water—over which a fixative is applied to prevent the paint from scaling off, or spotting when a drop of water touches it. In all Southwest rattles, the handle and the protruding tip of the stick should be painted red. Figure 94 shows three common Hopi designs for gourd rattles of the shape just described. In A, the main body of the rattle is either natural or painted white; the rain design is black except for a white line near the bottom as shown—rattles with this design play a prominent part in certain Hopi dances. The Hopi rattle shown in B is also very common: the gourd is painted white; the line around the middle is black, one-quarter inch wide; the round

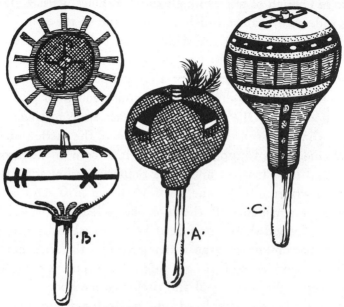

Fig. 94—*Hopi gourd-rattle designs.*

spot at the blossom end is green with the figure in black; out from this the lines are red and those at the handle end are also red. In the Hopi rattle shown in C the dark lines are black, some of them containing yellow spots; the blossom end is white; the squares in the middle are red and the neck red; between the two black lines above and below the red central squares is a yellow line.

Frequently three or four tiny fluffies are tied to a string and attached to the end of the stick at the blossom end, as shown in A, Figure 94. The string should be one to two inches long. Select colored fluffies to match the colors on the gourd.

Four typical Pueblo rattle designs are shown in Figure 95. The background color in all of these is brown; the designs are outlined in black and filled in with white, red, yellow, and green. On A, the figure shown is repeated on the opposite side; in B, the design is continuous, each figure being repeated four times; in C, each of the two figures is repeated twice; in D, the

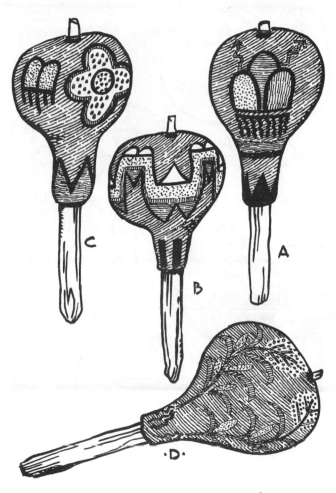

Fig. 95—*Pueblo gourd-rattle designs.*

corn figure is executed without black lines and is repeated three times.

Let us now take up the second type of Southwest gourd rattle. Although the type just described is common among the Hopis, the true ceremonial gourd rattle is of the shape shown in Figure 96. If gourds of this shape can be obtained, the mak-

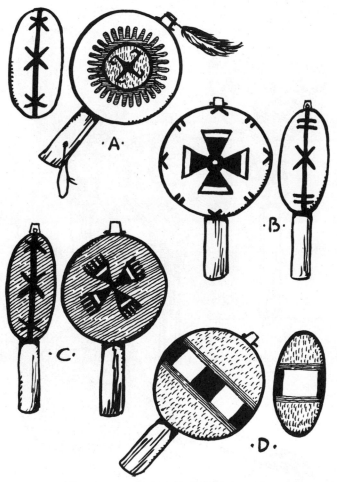

Fig. 96—*Hopi ceremonial gourd-rattles.*

ing is a simple task—merely bore a hole with a jackknife on the narrow edge and another hole directly opposite it, then insert the stick in the usual fashion. These rattles are held so as to move in the narrow dimension direction.

Figure 96 shows four authentic Hopi designs for such rattles. In A the gourd is painted white; the central spot is green edged with yellow, around which the black figure is painted as shown. In B, the gourd is white and the figure black and white. In C, the main body of the gourd is natural and unpainted, with the figure black and white. In D the top and bottom are pale blue, the central squares black and white, and the line above and below the squares, red.

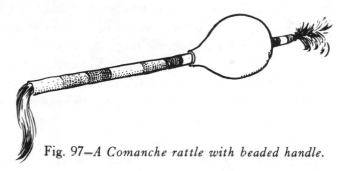

Fig. 97—*A Comanche rattle with beaded handle.*

Among the Comanches and Kiowas a common type of rattle is made with a smaller gourd with a handle about nine inches long as shown in Figure 97. The gourd is undecorated but the wood in the handle and tip is covered solidly with beading. Fluffies are attached to the tip and horse-hair to the end of the handle.

An unusual Zuni rattle is shown in Figure 98. This long,

ZUNI

slender gourd is painted yellow, the central line is black paralleled by lines of white and red as shown.

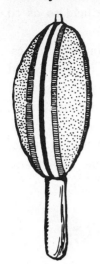

Fig. 98
An unusual Zuni gourd rattle.

A particularly interesting type of gourd-rattle decoration is shown in Figure 99. These gourds have no coloring at all but are decorated with tiny holes through the shell of the gourd made with a fine boring tool. That shown in A is from the Papago Indians, B from the Kawia, and C from California. The design on the Iowa rattle shown in D is created entirely by the tiny holes.

A collection of Cherokee (North Carolina) rattles are shown in Figure 100. It will be noted in A that these Indians do not use a stick handle in the large rattles but rely on the neck of the gourd as a handle; a hole is bored at the blossom end for the removal of the pith and seeds, and for the insertion of the pebbles, which is afterwards sealed by

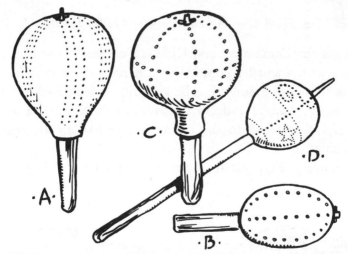

Fig. 99—*Gourd rattles decorated with holes through the shell.*

gluing a piece of rawhide or pasteboard to the gourd. B shows a tiny two-inch yellow gourd, unpainted, with a seven-inch

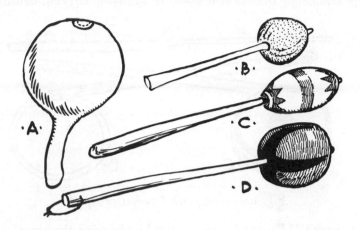

Fig. 100—*Cherokee Gourd Rattles*

handle. C is made from an egg-shaped gourd two and one-quarter inches in diameter with a twelve-inch handle; its design is in red. D is a small gourd three inches in diameter with a twelve-inch handle, decorated in black and red.

An unusual type of rattle made from the neck of a gourd is shown in Figure 101. This is from the Senecas. A wooden disc is fitted into the large end, in the center of which a hole is bored to receive the end of the stick.

On all of these types of gourd rattles a tuft of colored fluffies may be tied to the end of the stick as shown in A, Figure 96.

Drumstick Rattles

Drumstick rattles serve a double purpose — they are among the best of dance-rattles to carry

Fig. 101
Dance-rattle from the neck of a gourd.

in the dancer's hands, and are a unique and very effective type of drumstick when used by the drummers. Figure 102 shows the appearance of one of these—it is really a curved drumstick

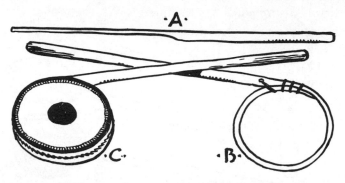

Fig. 102—*Chippewa Drumstick Rattle*

(Chapter VII) turned into a rattle by covering the circular end with rawhide as in making a drum, inside of which pebbles are placed. When used as a drumstick the clicking of the rattles can be distinctly heard between the booms of the drum, thus not only creating an interesting sound effect but producing half beats or quarter beats that never fail to give added stimulus to the dancer's movements.

To make the rattle a stick of black ash or white oak is needed, secured from the trunk of a sapling as described in Chapter VII. It should be three-quarters inch wide and twenty-eight inches long. One-half its length is to serve as the handle and the other fourteen inches is to be bent into the circular end. The handle part should be whittled down to a round stick one-half inch in diameter or less. The section to be bent remains at its full width, three-quarters inch, but is thinned down to a thickness of one-quarter inch—A in Figure 102 shows the side view of the stick. Soak the stick in water for a few hours and then bend the end into the hoop and bind securely with wet rawhide thongs as shown in B. To forestall any possibility of its losing its shape, bore a hole through the stick as shown in **B**, run a thong through and tie.

Scraps of rawhide left over from making a drum will supply the little "drumheads" for the hoop. Tack them over the frame temporarily just as in making a hand-drum (Chapter III) and then sew the two heads together along the edges as shown in **C**, using a darning needle and string. Put a small handful of tiny pebbles and a few kernels of corn inside.

When used as a drumstick, the circular side (the section away from the handle) should be struck against the drum as indicated in Figure 89.

The rawhide is painted by the same methods described for painting drums in Chapter III. Figure 102 shows a Chippewa decoration—the center spot is blue, and the outer line is blue edged on the inside with a thin line of yellow. The opposite side is the same except that the colors are reversed. Figure 103 shows two other Chippewa drumstick rattles; the two sides of the rattle shown in A have the figures in red; B shows the

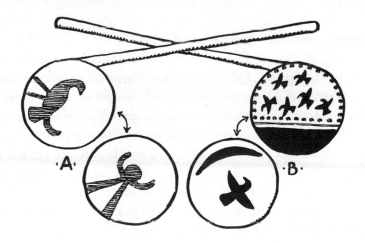

Fig. 103—*Chippewa designs for Drumstick Rattles.*

two sides of another rattle—the moon and bird on the one side are blue, the birds on the other are blue, the solid area at the bottom blue, the line and dots red.

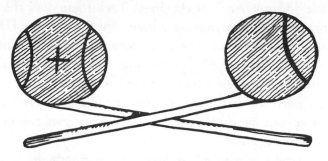

Fig. 104—*Plains Indian drumstick rattle designs.*

A Plains Indian drumstick rattle is shown in Figure 104. The rawhide is painted solid yellow with the fine lines in blue.

Rawhide Rattles

Next to gourds the most prevalent and widely used dance-rattles were made of rawhide. These were extensively employed by the many tribes of the Plains, and occasionally by the Chippewas, but were less often seen among the Eastern Woodland Indians. Rawhide rattles are excellent rhythmic instruments in the hands of dancers and are second only to gourds in the strength and the pleasantness of the sound they produce.

The typical rawhide rattle varies in detail as one goes from tribe to tribe but the general construction is the same. Figure 105, C, shows the usual Plains Indian style. Secure a piece of heavy rawhide five inches by nine inches in size, preferably from neck or shoulders of the animal since the hide there is thicker and will produce a rattle that will keep its shape better, particularly if it should become wet.

Soak the rawhide for several hours to soften it. With a pencil mark the pattern shown in A, Figure 105, on the hide and cut out along these lines. We now have a piece of hide in the shape of a figure-of-eight with a half-inch hole between the two circular halves—fold this at the middle placing one of the circular pieces over the other thus making a double layer of hide, and sew the edges together very securely with heavy linen thread. Continue the sewing all around except for a one-inch opening directly opposite the half-inch hole, at which point the sewing should be stopped but long threads left with which to complete it later. Now turn the bag thus formed inside out so that the sewed edges are inside. If the hide becomes dry as you work, dip it in water.

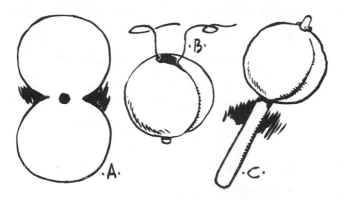

Fig. 105—*Making a rawhide rattle.*

Now we must fill the rawhide sack with fine, dry sand. When it is partly full, put a temporary wooden plug or wad of cloth in the half-inch hole and continue to add sand in the unsewed opening, packing it down with a stick and continuing to add more sand until the rawhide is forced into a round ball and will hold no more, as shown in B, Figure 105. Rub the outside with your hands and work out all bumps and irregularities. Then hang it up by the threads in the sun to dry.

When the rawhide has thoroughly dried remove the plug

and pour out the sand—the round hollow shell of rawhide will now keep its shape permanently. Whittle a smooth round stick nine or ten inches long and three-quarters inch thick for the handle as shown in C—it should have a slight shoulder at the bottom of the rawhide to prevent the globe from slipping. Before the stick is put in, place the bottom of the rawhide shell in a saucer of water for a few minutes to soften the hide around the bottom hole where the sewing must be completed. Then put a handful of small pebbles and a few kernels of corn or other seeds inside, insert the stick in the holes, sew up the bottom hole tightly against the stick, wrap the ends of the thread around the stick and tie. Bore a small hole through the stick next to the rawhide at the top, insert a peg in it, and the rattle is finished.

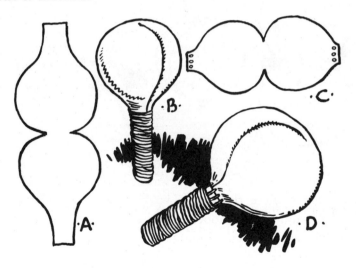

Fig. 106—*Other methods of making rawhide rattles.*

Another common type of Plains Indian rawhide rattle, still easier to make, does not have a stick extending all the way through it but merely extending into the bottom hole. Such rattles are shown in Figure 106. The pattern for B is shown in A. These rattles vary from three to six inches in diameter and

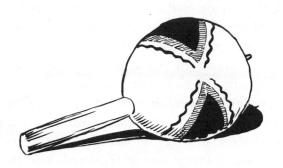

Fig. 107—*A Sioux rawhide rattle, painted.*

the pattern should be planned for the size desired. Fold the two layers together and sew up the edges as before, continuing the sewing down to the narrow sections at the bottom. Fill with sand as described above and let dry. When the sand has been removed soften the unsewed parts at the bottom in a bowl of water. Make a wooden handle three-quarters inch thick and six inches long. Insert the stick one inch up into the globe of the rattle, then fold the narrow sections of the hide around it and sew together very tightly, trimming off the edges if they overlap. To complete the rattle, wrap a wet rawhide thong around the handle throughout its entire length as shown in B.

A similar type of rattle from the Wichita Indians is illustrated in D, Figure 106, the pattern for which is shown in C. It

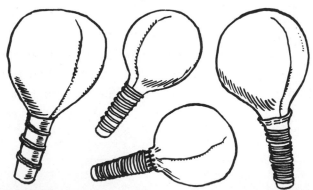

is made like the preceding rattle except that it is held to the stick in a different way: Cut four to six small holes through the rawhide at the bottom edge of the globe, through which six-inch rawhide thongs are run. These thongs are pulled half way through the holes, then doubled down on the handle and bound to the handle by wrapping it solidly throughout its length with a wet rawhide thong.

Fig. 108
*A Chippewa rattle
with holes punched
through the
rawhide.*

Decorating Rawhide Rattles.—More often than not rawhide rattles are left undecorated, but one occasionally sees one that is nicely ornamented with painted designs, as, for example, the old Sioux rattle in Figure 107. The inner triangle is red, the outer one blue, and the wavy line black. The balance of the rattle is natural. Dry paint powder mixed with a little water and a few drops of glue to make a thin paste should be used, and applied to the dry rawhide.

Occasionally an old-time rawhide rattle is seen among the Chippewas decorated by means of holes punched through the rawhide as shown in Figure 108. The holes must be put in before the rawhide is sewed up and can be produced with any pointed instrument or by driving a good sized nail through the hide.

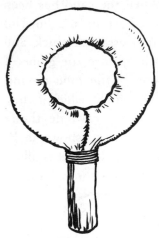

Fig. 109
*A Sioux Doughnut-shaped
Rawhide Rattle.*

Doughnut-Shaped Rawhide Rattle.—An oddity in rattles is seen in the doughnut-shaped affair from the Sioux pictured in Figure 109. A strip

of very heavy rawhide twenty inches long and four inches wide
will be needed, slightly wider at the ends to furnish a projection
of rawhide over which thongs can be wrapped in binding the
rawhide to the handle. From the principles of rawhide rattle
construction already set forth, the method of constructing this
type can be easily worked out.

Steer-Horn Rattles

From a section of a steer's horn an excellent dance-rattle
may be made of the type shown in Figure 110. Saw off a four-
inch section from the large end of the horn, and scrape it to
smooth it up. Broken glass is the most effective means of scraping horn, after which fine sandpaper is used, and finally pumice
stone. If the horn is boiled in water for a half hour it can be
scraped much more easily. From cedar, basswood, or other soft
wood, carefully whittle two plugs that will fit snugly into the
ends of the horn and close them tightly. Fasten these plugs in
place with brass-headed tacks as shown. Now bore a hole in
each wooden end one-quarter inch in diameter, put a handful
of tiny pebbles and some seeds into the rattle,
and then insert the handle as shown. The handle
is made fast by a shoulder at the bottom and a
peg forced through a small hole bored through
the stick at the top.

A nicely polished horn will need no decoration
other than the brass-headed tacks and the tuft
of fluffies tied to the top of the stick with a string
as shown in Figure 110.

Birch-Bark Rattles

Birch-bark—that beautiful, thick, pliable "parfleche" of the woods, water-proof, decay-proof,
worm-proof, destructible only by fire—was used

Fig. 110
*Steer-horn
Dance-rattle.*

by the Woodland Indians for the making of countless objects for use in the daily run of life. Without it, life for these roamers of the forests would have been different indeed, and much more difficult. Among other things they made from it pots, pans, cups, baskets, boxes, quivers, arm-guards, wigwam roofs, wrapping paper—and *dance-rattles*.

From thick, heavy birch-bark, cut a rectangular piece ten inches long and five inches wide by means of a pair of tin-shears. Take this from a fallen or dead birch tree—do not strip it from a living tree unless you are far back in the uninhabited wilds, and in that case, only from a large tree a foot or more in diameter, a tree of which size will not be killed by the removal of bark as will a smaller one. Coil the bark into the shape of the rattle (Figure 111), putting the yellow side out and the white side (the side which is exposed on the tree) in—the yellow or inner side of the bark is much more firm and tough and is always used for the outside of baskets and similar objects. The overlapped edges of the coiled piece of bark must be laced together and that offers somewhat of a problem: Punch holes through the two layers every half inch as indicated in Figure 111 and insert a couple of wooden pegs through them to hold the bark temporarily. Now some sort of lacing should be run through the holes, as illustrated, to hold the bark together permanently—the Indian would use a slender strip or thong from the inner bark of basswood for this, which produces the strongest and most enduring of string or lacing. Failing to find this, a thong of wet rawhide may be used, or, if need be, the bark can be held together with copper rivets.

Fig. 111
Chippewa
Birch-bark
Dance-rattle.

Now two discs must be whittled out of soft wood just large

enough so that they will fit snugly into the ends. In the center of these the holes are bored to receive the stick. With the discs in place, tack the bark to them with small tacks, drop in a handful of pebbles and a few kernels of corn, insert the stick and make secure by a peg through the small end as shown. A tuft of colored fluffies may be added.

Turtle-Shell Rattles

Excellent rattles were made from turtle shells by many Indian tribes, particularly those of the Eastern Woodlands. The huge turtle rattles of the Iroquois made from shells often over a foot in length, looked for all the world like a living turtle since the head of the turtle was incorporated as the end of the short handle—these rattles were an essential part of the equipment for the solid-face or mask dances for which this tribe was famous. Most tribes, however, used small turtles not over four or five inches in length.

After the turtle has been killed and the shell thoroughly cleaned out, it should be placed in the sun for a few days to dry and cure. If the odor does not leave it after drying, hang it for a few hours in wood smoke over a smoldering fire. The stick for the handle should be of soft wood about nine inches in length. The handle end should be whittled down to a round stick one-half to three-quarters inch thick, but the rattle end should fan out to a flat paddle just large enough to fit into the large opening of the shell. The whittling should be done carefully and the paddle end caused to fit very snugly and tightly.

After a handful of pebbles and a few peas, kernels of corn, or grains of wheat are placed inside, we are ready to lace the upper and lower shells together. Drill or burn two small holes near the handle end through the two layers of shell and the wooden stick within, as indicated in A, Figure 112. Run a wet rawhide thong through these holes and tie on the belly side of the turtle. Now burn or drill holes through the two layers of shell at the other end and close the opening by running wet thongs of rawhide or wire through these holes and pulling the lower lip up tightly against the upper shell—two or three of these holes will suffice.

The handle should extend out from the shell about five inches. While usually left plain, it may be ornamented by carving the end to represent a turtle head.

Turtle-shell Leg Rattles.—Another type of turtle rattle common among the Plains and Southwest Indians is worn around the leg, usually just below the knee. Two types of these are shown in B and C, Figure 112, both from the Pueblos. The rattle sound is produced by attachments to the shell rather than pebbles within it—these dangles were usually dew-claws or hoof bells in the old days, but in more recent years use has also been made of the tin tinkles described on page 195 and illustrated in Figure 118. Since tin is easy to find and the other items rare, the tinkles are recommended.

In B, Figure 112, the tinkles are tied to a leather thong run through two holes drilled or burned through the back of the shell as shown, the thong being long enough to tie around the leg. In C, the tinkles are tied through small holes burned or drilled along the lower edge of the shell; the thong for tying the rattle to the leg in this case is merely run through the center between the upper and lower shells.

Place these rattles on the back of the leg just below the knee, and tie to the leg with the thong.

Wooden Rattles

The Indians of the Northwest Coast made rattles from two hollowed out shells of wood laced together with thongs of rawhide. These they decorated with carving, giving them the characteristic totem effect that all the ornamentation that these

Indians use. A striking array of carved designs appears on the rattles in this area, all demonstrating the skill of these Indians in carving. Two samples of simple Northwest rattles are shown in Figure 113.

It will be noted that the usual stick handle is used in these rattles. Tiny holes are bored along the edges of the wooden shells and laces of rawhide run through them to tie the two halves together. The carving of the faces is a more difficult task than is encountered in any other type of rattle making, especially for people inexperienced in wood-carving. If basswood or white pine is used it can be accomplished with an ordinary jackknife, although a set of small wood-carving tools is always desirable. The carved faces are in low relief and reliance placed

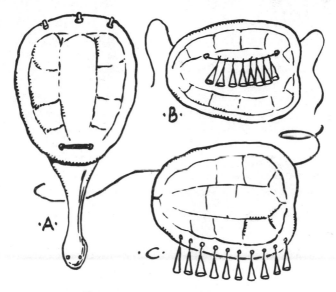

Fig. 112—*Turtle-shell Rattles.*

on painting to bring out the features. The background is left in the natural wood color, with the features in black highlighted with red. Inside the rattle are the usual pebbles.

A wooden rattle from the Chippewas is shown in Figure 114. These are rare among the Woodland tribes. This consists of two hollowed-out shells of wood glued together at the point indicated by the line on the drawing. The handle fits snugly and is firmly pegged at the top. The Chippewa Indian would hollow

Fig. 113—*Carved wooden rattles from the northwest coast.*

out these wooden shells with the aid of his crooked knife which is an ideal implement for such a task as this.

Sea-Shell Rattles

The Hiada Indians made dance-rattles from sea-shells as shown in Figure 115. Select a shell of the shape illustrated that is about five inches across—both halves of the shell will be needed, of course. The handle section of the stick is round but the rattle end is sawed down the center and then thinned down with a jackknife, thus creating two flat, pliable strips between which the shell is forced. The split section should extend to within a quarter of an inch of the end of the shell. Two holes are then bored through the shells either side of the stick and within a half inch of its end, through which a wet rawhide thong is run and tied tightly, binding the two ends of the split stick firmly

to the shell, as shown in Figure 115. Holes are frequently bored through the shells a half inch from the edges as illustrated, these serving no purpose other than decoration. The usual handful of pebbles and seeds is put inside.

Tin-Can Rattles

During the past seventy-five years the Indians of the Plains and Woodlands have accepted the baking-powder can as their own and have made from it excellent dance-rattles. This is understandable, for the can comes ready-made and all that needs to be done is to put inside a handful of pebbles

Fig. 114
A Chippewa Wooden Rattle.

and a few seeds such as corn, wheat, or wild rice, and then to insert a wooden handle. And there is nothing second-rate about these can rattles, as the Indian sees it, and they are used in many ancient dances. For some dances tradition prescribes the use of certain types of rattles that have been associated with these ceremonies throughout the years, long before the tin can was known, but there are many others for which the can is perfectly acceptable and commonly used.

Figure 116 shows the construction of the baking-powder can rattle — merely punch holes in the middle of the bottom and the lid, put the pebbles and

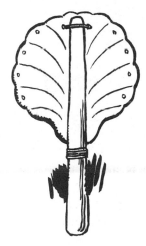

Fig. 115
A sea-shell rattle.

seeds inside, insert the wooden handle and peg it at the top. Two designs taken from Indian rattles are suggested in Figure 116. Special care must be taken in painting tin to see that it is

Fig. 116—*Tin-can rattles.*

completely covered, since any little spots left unpainted will reflect light and publish their presence.

Cocoanut Rattles

In recent years the Creek Indians have made rattles from cocoanuts by the same method used for gourds. Two holes are bored, one in each end, and the contents removed. A stick handle is inserted through the two holes and held by a peg at the top, as in making gourd rattles. A thoroughly dried cocoanut makes an excellent rattle.

Hoof, Bone, and Tin Rattles

In the old days the Indians of the Plains and Southwest

areas made rattles by attaching little bell-shaped affairs made from the hoofs of animals to sticks of wood. Sometimes these were tied along the side of a stick as shown in Figure 117, and

Fig. 117—*Hoof rattles.*

again were bunched at the end of the stick. Dew-claws were often used in the same way. Both of these materials are hard to obtain in craft work today and of late the Indians themselves have frequently substituted tin tinkles for the claws and hoofs. These tin tinkles are used in many ways by the Indians, particularly in ornamenting clothing.

The tin tinkles are made from triangular pieces of tin as shown in A, Figure 118, about three-quarters inch high and one and three-quarters inches wide at the bottom. Larger tinkles may be made following these proportions and will of course make more noise. A knot is tied at the end of a buckskin thong and placed over the tin as shown; then the tin is bent into the cone shape shown in B with a pair of pliers. The buckskin thongs are then attached to the stick to make the rattle shown in Figure 117, this stick being about fifteen inches long, one inch wide, and three-eighths to one-half inch thick. Holes may be

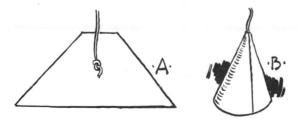

Fig. 118—*Making a tin tinkle.*

made along the stick through which the thongs are run and held with a knot on the back side, or the thongs may be tacked to the stick with small brass-headed tacks. The tinkles should hang down about one inch from the stick. A rattle of this type should have from twenty-five to thirty-five of the tin tinkles.

In Indian crafts in camps and clubs today, chicken and turkey bones are frequently substituted for hoofs and claws, and are easier to prepare than the tin tinkles. Wing and leg bones are needed—clean them, dry them well in the sun, and cut them into uniform lengths of about two inches. Run a buckskin thong through the center of each and tie a knot at the end large enough to prevent the bone from slipping off. Attach the bones to the stick as described for assembling the rattle of tin tinkles in the preceding paragraph. At least twenty-five bones will be needed for a good rattle.

Rattles from Any Old Thing

Thus far all the rattles discussed have been authentic Indian ones, but we need not confine ourselves to these in children's crafts and music classes today, for there is a great array of boxes, cans, and cartons, to be picked up on every hand, that will make excellent rattles, so many in fact that no two children will need to make the same kind. Once one gets the idea of the use of small boxes and cans for rattles he will find himself picking them up in numbers and in a wide variety of shapes. In a rhythm band the more different types of rattles there are, the greater will be the interest.

The sources are *tin, cardboard* and *wood:*

We have already seen the use the Indian made of the baking-powder can in making dance-rattles that in recent years have been accepted by them as appropriate for certain types of dances. There are many other types of cans that can be turned into rattles by exactly the same methods as described for the baking-powder can—little *cinnamon cans, all-spice cans, mustard cans, paprika cans, nutmeg cans, condensed-milk cans, coughdrop cans, typewriter-ribbon cans, round cigarette tins, flat cigarette tins, talcum-powder cans,* and so on and so on without end. The side of the can through which the stick should be inserted depends on the shape of the can and position of the lid—a little ingenuity will always solve this problem.

Not only cans but cardboard boxes and cartons may be used for rattles—little *pill boxes,* both round and rectangular, *safety-match boxes,* pint and quart *ice cream cartons, table-salt boxes* —in fact any square, rectangular, or round box up to six or seven inches in size. Glue the lid to the box, insert the stick, and peg the end or hold with a wrapping of several layers of string around the end, as described for making authentic Indian rattles.

HOOF
RATT

Small wooden boxes may also be utilized. A half-size cigar box (one made to hold twenty-five cigars), or the very small boxes that contain a dozen small-sized cigars, make excellent rattles.

Rattles of different appearance may be made from boxes of the same shape and size by inserting the stick from different directions. An example is seen in the two illustrations of the paprika-box rattle on page 199.

Paint the rattles in Indian designs and interesting effects will be produced that will completely conceal the nature of the box within.

MORACHES

Moraches or *guayos* are scraping instruments consisting of a notched stick over which another stick is rubbed to the rhythm of the dancing, thus producing an intriguing addition to the rhythmic booming and clicking of the percussion instruments such as drums and rattles. Figure 119 shows a typical

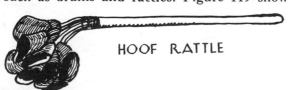
HOOF RATTLE

morache of simple type. In using it the Indian squats down beside a resonator of some type such as an inverted basket, places one end of the notched stick on it, and holding the other end in his hand, rubs the round stick up and down it with the other hand, the resonator serving as an amplifier that greatly increases the sound, as well as giving it an interesting tone quality. Used as an accompaniment to the drums, the morache is a fascinating instrument for Indian and other types of dancing that rely on percussion; in the council ring it is a particularly favored time-beater for Indian ceremonies; for recreational use it plays an important part in rhythm bands. The morache was widely used by the various Indian tribes of the Plains and Southwest.

Fig. 119—*Morache or Guayo.*

To make the morache a stick is needed of any kind of wood that is not too hard to whittle yet not so soft that the notches will split, measuring twenty to twenty-four inches in length, about two inches in width, and one-half inch in thickness. The edge that is to be notched should be thinned down slightly, say to five-sixteenths inch in thickness. The notches should be a half inch deep, about three-eighths inch wide and spaced one-half inch or less apart. All edges should be slightly rounded off. The scraping stick should be round, three-quarters inch thick, and eight to ten inches long. Figure 119 shows both the finished morache and the rubbing stick.

For a resonator the Southwest Indians used an inverted basket of the shape of a mixing bowl, a half of a gourd, or a

whole gourd. The Plains Indians used a piece of parfleche or folded rawhide. Today we can use a large gourd, a small packing box, a galvanized bucket or kettle, a washbasin, or any similar object; or if none of these can be obtained, a thin board may be placed over a hole or ditch in the ground, which method was sometimes used by the Southwest Indians when suitable objects were not near at hand.

To play the morache, kneel beside the inverted resonator, place one end of the notched stick on the upturned bottom, hold the other end in the left hand, and rub the scraping stick up and down to the rhythm of the drumming. The downward stroke is made more sharply and with more pressure than the upward stroke.

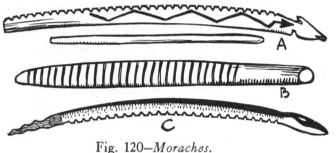

Fig. 120—*Moraches.*

A slightly different type of morache is shown in B, Figure 120. The stick is of the same shape and dimensions as in the other style, but has the notches on the broad side rather than the edge.

Sometimes the moraches or guayos were highly decorated. Figure 120, A and C, shows carved and painted sticks, that in C being in the form of a snake.

BULLROARERS

A bullroarer is a thin feather-shaped piece of wood which, when whirled in the air by means of an attached string, gives a loud humming or roaring sound. Symbolizing the thunder,

these roaring sticks are used in certain ceremonial dances in the Southwest, and imitations of the ritualistic ones are often used as playthings by children. Bullroarers are unusually intriguing instruments and, while they can scarcely be called percussion instruments, yet they provide a delightful accompaniment for drums and rattles, emitting as they do a constant roar as a background for the staccato booming of tomtoms.

A piece of light soft wood is needed, 13 inches long, 2 inches wide, and one-fourth inch thick. The stick is first whittled to the shape shown in Figure 121, being narrowed down at the string end to an inch and a quarter. The bottom side of the stick remains flat, while the top side has all the edges beveled or rounded down to a thin edge; that is, the stick remains at full width at the center but near the edges it is thinned down to a sharp edge. Bore a hole at the square end, through which the end of a three-foot string is tied. Too light a string will break when the bullroarer is whirled and too heavy a one will not permit the roarer to spin fast enough to produce the sound. The best results are obtained by using four strands of ordinary string rather than one heavy cord. Sometimes a ring is attached to the end of the string through which the finger may be inserted in order to hold it more securely while swinging it.

To use the bullroarer, wrap the end of the string around the forefinger, or insert the finger through the ring, and whirl the roarer in the air in a circle in front of the body. After so using it for a moment and the string becomes twisted, allow it to stop and immediately start whirling it in the opposite direction. If a steady roar is wanted, use two bullroarers each handled by a different person, and start the second one a moment after the first has been started; when the first one is stopped to change directions, the second one will still be going.

To decorate the bullroarer in Southwest Indian fashion, paint it white with the lightning symbol in black as shown in

B. Figure 121, or paint it black with the lightning symbol in white as in C. This design in white on black symbolizes the lightning against the background of a storm cloud.

When not in use as a bullroarer, this instrument makes a

Fig. 121—*Bullroarers.*

good weather vane when suspended from a crossbar or limb. It whirls and spins constantly in the breeze and indicates the direction of the wind.

DANCING BELLS

Bells worn by the dancers are always a strong incentive to dancing—they supply an added inspiration, an increased desire to move, a will to dance and to cause the bells to jingle. They are a very definite aid to beginners in learning to dance, helping them to sense the rhythm, to move in time to it, and to feel in harmony with it. The Indian loves his dancing bells and prizes them highly. One of the chief appeals of the Indian dance-drama is the loud jingling of dancing bells to the virile, masculine movements of robust dancers—minus bells the Redman's dancing would definitely lose an important element in spectator appeal. Bells are strongly recommended for all forms of Indian dancing, both in practice and recital.

In the old days the Indians made bells from the hoofs of animals, but in the last seventy-five years have taken to themselves with avid delight the white man's sleighbells. The bigger the bells the better they are liked, for large bells mean a louder sound and usually a more pleasing one. The Indian cuts the long strings of bells into sections and ties them around his ankles or legs, or attaches them to his body in other ways. The graduated strings of heavy brass sleighbells of varying sizes and sounds are the favored types, because they permit the Indian to combine the bells in such a way that those on one leg produce a different sound from those on the other. Thus when he dances there is a noticeable difference in tone produced by each of his feet.

Unhappily, sleighbells are becoming more and more scarce but they can still be obtained if one goes on the hunt for them. Old ones can be found hanging in the barns and sheds of farmers throughout the north country and, since sleighing days are over for most of those farmers, they will usually part with them willingly. If the straps of these old bells have rotted, as will usually be the case, they should be restrung on new leather, otherwise the rough usage they necessarily receive in dancing will soon pull loose the bells. New bells can be purchased from large wholesale hardware stores.

Sleighbells are used by dancers in three ways—(1) around the ankles or legs just below the knees, (2) around the waist as a belt, and (3) extending down the sides of the thighs from the belt bells to the knee bells. Strong dancers frequently use all these types at the same time. Occasionally one sees an Indian with an additional string of bells hung over his shoulder.

The more essential strings of bells for dancing are those that go around the ankles or legs below the knees. If the bells are small a string should be used that will wrap around the ankle or leg two or three times. In the case of large bells, four or five to a leg are sufficient. Cut the long string of sleighbells into the desired lengths depending on the size of the bells, tie strips of cloth to the ends of each, wrap around the ankle or leg, and fasten by tying the ends of the cloth together. The waist bells are prepared with cloth ends in the same way. The vertical leg bells are attached by tying one of the cloth ends to the string of waist bells and the other end to that of the knee bells.

Another type of bell sometimes used in Indian dancing is the turkey bell obtainable from any large hardware store. Two or three of these are attached to each wrist.

Tinkles and Bells for Clothing

Cone-shaped tin tinkles constructed as described on page 195 are a common ornamentation on the clothing of Plains Indians. They are particularly favored by women as fringes for skirts and blouses. Men use them down the sides of the leggings and as fringes for their vests or shirts. A quantity of these tinkles on a dancer's clothing can be heard much more distinctly than one might imagine.

Tin tinkles are also frequently employed on arm bands. A couple of dozen of them are tied along a thong of buckskin which is then fastened around the arm above the elbow.

The little inexpensive bells of the sleighbell type that are sold in five-and-ten-cent stores, toy stores, and theatrical stores, while too small and ineffective for dancing leg bells, are excellent for use on a dancer's clothing. Sewed in rows down the sides of leggings, on breechcloths and on shirts, these little bells produce a soft tinkling sound and at the same time serve as an appropriate ornamentation.

SELECTED BIBLIOGRAPHY OF INDIAN DANCING AND MUSIC

Popular Books on Indian Dancing

Barrett, S. A. *Dream Dance of the Chippewa and Menominee Indians*. Milwaukee: Milwaukee Public Museum, 1911.

Buttree, Julia M. *The Rhythm of the Redman*. New York: A. S. Barnes and Company, 1930.

Evans, Bessie and May E. *American Indian Dance Steps*. New York: A. S. Barnes and Company, 1931.

Salomon, Julian Harris. *The Book of Indian Crafts and Indian Lore*. New York: Harper and Brothers, 1928.

Schwendener, Norma and Tibbels, Averil. *Legends and Dances of Old Mexico*. New York: A. S. Barnes and Company, 1934.

Seton, Ernest Thompson. *The Birch Bark Roll of Woodcraft*, Activities Section. New York: A. S. Barnes and Company, 1931.

Seton, Ernest Thompson. *The Book of Woodcraft*. Garden City: Garden City Publishing Company, 1921.

Indian Music

Alexander, Hartley. *Manito Masks*. New York: E. P. Dutton and Company, 1925.

Burton, Frederick Russell. *American Primitive Music*. New York: Muffat, Yard and Company, 1909.

Buttree, Julia M. *The Rhythm of the Redman*. New York: A. S. Barnes and Company, 1930.

Cronyn, George William. *The Path of the Rainbow*. New York: Boni and Liveright, 1918.

Curtis, Natalie. *The Indians' Book*. New York: Harper and Brothers, 1937. (Dover reprint)

Densmore, Frances. *Cheyenne and Arapaho Music*. Los Angeles: Southwest Museum, 1936.

Chippewa Music (2 Volumes). Bureau of American Ethnology Bulletins 45 and 53. Washington: Government Printing Office, 1910 and 1913.

Indian Action Songs. Boston: C. C. Birchard and Company, 1921.

Mandan and Hidasta Music. Bureau of American Ethnology Bulletin 80. Washington: Government Printing Office, 1923.

Menominee Music. Bureau of American Ethnology Bulletin 102. Washington: Government Printing Office, 1932.

Northern Ute Music. Bureau of American Ethnology Bulletin 75. Washington: Government Printing Office, 1922.

Papago Music. Bureau of American Ethnology Bulletin 90. Washington: Government Printing Office, 1929.

Pawnee Music. Bureau of American Ethnology Bulletin 93. Washington: Government Printing Office, 1929.

Teton Sioux Music. Bureau of American Ethnology Bulletin 61. Washington: Government Printing Office, 1918.

Yuman and Yaqui Music. Bureau of American Ethnology Bulletin 110. Washington: Government Printing Office, 1932.

Evans, Bessie and May E. *American Indian Dance Steps*. New York: A. S. Barnes and Company, 1931.

Fletcher, Alice C. *Indian Games and Dances with Native Songs*. Boston: C. C. Birchard and Company, 1915.

Indian Story and Song from North America. Boston: Small, Maynard and Company, 1900.

The Hako; A Pawnee Ceremony. Bureau of American Ethnology Annual Report, 1900. Washington: Government Printing Office, 1904.

Fletcher, Alice C. and LaFlesche, Francis. *The Omaha Tribe.* Bureau of American Ethnology, Annual Report, 1905. Washington: Government Printing Office, 1911.

Gilman, B. I. *Hopi Songs.* Boston: Houghton-Mifflin Co., 1908.

Hoffman, W. J. *The Mide'winwin or "Grand Medicine Society" of the Ojibway.* Bureau of American Ethnology, 7th Annual Report. Washington: Government Printing Office.

Salomon, Julian Harris. *The Book of Indian Crafts and Indian Lore.* New York: Harper and Brothers, 1928.

Index

Index — Continued

A CATALOGUE OF SELECTED DOVER BOOKS
IN ALL FIELDS OF INTEREST

A CATALOGUE OF SELECTED DOVER BOOKS
IN ALL FIELDS OF INTEREST

AMERICA'S OLD MASTERS, James T. Flexner. Four men emerged unexpectedly from provincial 18th century America to leadership in European art: Benjamin West, J. S. Copley, C. R. Peale, Gilbert Stuart. Brilliant coverage of lives and contributions. Revised, 1967 edition. 69 plates. 365pp. of text.

21806-6 Paperbound $3.00

FIRST FLOWERS OF OUR WILDERNESS: AMERICAN PAINTING, THE COLONIAL PERIOD, James T. Flexner. Painters, and regional painting traditions from earliest Colonial times up to the emergence of Copley, West and Peale Sr., Foster, Gustavus Hesselius, Feke, John Smibert and many anonymous painters in the primitive manner. Engaging presentation, with 162 illustrations. xxii + 368pp.

22180-6 Paperbound $3.50

THE LIGHT OF DISTANT SKIES: AMERICAN PAINTING, 1760-1835, James T. Flexner. The great generation of early American painters goes to Europe to learn and to teach: West, Copley, Gilbert Stuart and others. Allston, Trumbull, Morse; also contemporary American painters—primitives, derivatives, academics—who remained in America. 102 illustrations. xiii + 306pp.

22179-2 Paperbound $3.00

A HISTORY OF THE RISE AND PROGRESS OF THE ARTS OF DESIGN IN THE UNITED STATES, William Dunlap. Much the richest mine of information on early American painters, sculptors, architects, engravers, miniaturists, etc. The only source of information for scores of artists, the major primary source for many others. Unabridged reprint of rare original 1834 edition, with new introduction by James T. Flexner, and 394 new illustrations. Edited by Rita Weiss. $6\frac{5}{8}$ x $9\frac{5}{8}$.

21695-0, 21696-9, 21697-7 Three volumes, Paperbound $13.50

EPOCHS OF CHINESE AND JAPANESE ART, Ernest F. Fenollosa. From primitive Chinese art to the 20th century, thorough history, explanation of every important art period and form, including Japanese woodcuts; main stress on China and Japan, but Tibet, Korea also included. Still unexcelled for its detailed, rich coverage of cultural background, aesthetic elements, diffusion studies, particularly of the historical period. 2nd, 1913 edition. 242 illustrations. lii + 439pp. of text.

20364-6, 20365-4 Two volumes, Paperbound $6.00

THE GENTLE ART OF MAKING ENEMIES, James A. M. Whistler. Greatest wit of his day deflates Oscar Wilde, Ruskin, Swinburne; strikes back at inane critics, exhibitions, art journalism; aesthetics of impressionist revolution in most striking form. Highly readable classic by great painter. Reproduction of edition designed by Whistler. Introduction by Alfred Werner. xxxvi + 334pp.

21875-9 Paperbound $2.50

DESIGN BY ACCIDENT; A BOOK OF "ACCIDENTAL EFFECTS" FOR ARTISTS AND DESIGNERS, James F. O'Brien. Create your own unique, striking, imaginative effects by "controlled accident" interaction of materials: paints and lacquers, oil and water based paints, splatter, crackling materials, shatter, similar items. Everything you do will be different; first book on this limitless art, so useful to both fine artist and commercial artist. Full instructions. 192 plates showing "accidents," 8 in color. viii + 215pp. 8⅜ x 11¼.   21942-9 Paperbound $3.50

THE BOOK OF SIGNS, Rudolf Koch. Famed German type designer draws 493 beautiful symbols: religious, mystical, alchemical, imperial, property marks, runes, etc. Remarkable fusion of traditional and modern. Good for suggestions of timelessness, smartness, modernity. Text. vi + 104pp. 6⅛ x 9¼.
                                                20162-7 Paperbound $1.25

HISTORY OF INDIAN AND INDONESIAN ART, Ananda K. Coomaraswamy. An unabridged republication of one of the finest books by a great scholar in Eastern art. Rich in descriptive material, history, social backgrounds; Sunga reliefs, Rajput paintings, Gupta temples, Burmese frescoes, textiles, jewelry, sculpture, etc. 400 photos. viii + 423pp. 6⅜ x 9¾.   21436-2 Paperbound $4.00

PRIMITIVE ART, Franz Boas. America's foremost anthropologist surveys textiles, ceramics, woodcarving, basketry, metalwork, etc.; patterns, technology, creation of symbols, style origins. All areas of world, but very full on Northwest Coast Indians. More than 350 illustrations of baskets, boxes, totem poles, weapons, etc. 378 pp.
                                                20025-6 Paperbound $3.00

THE GENTLEMAN AND CABINET MAKER'S DIRECTOR, Thomas Chippendale. Full reprint (third edition, 1762) of most influential furniture book of all time, by master cabinetmaker. 200 plates, illustrating chairs, sofas, mirrors, tables, cabinets, plus 24 photographs of surviving pieces. Biographical introduction by N. Bienenstock. vi + 249pp. 9⅞ x 12¾.   21601-2 Paperbound $4.00

AMERICAN ANTIQUE FURNITURE, Edgar G. Miller, Jr. The basic coverage of all American furniture before 1840. Individual chapters cover type of furniture—clocks, tables, sideboards, etc.—chronologically, with inexhaustible wealth of data. More than 2100 photographs, all identified, commented on. Essential to all early American collectors. Introduction by H. E. Keyes. vi + 1106pp. 7⅞ x 10¾.
                                21599-7, 21600-4 Two volumes, Paperbound $11.00

PENNSYLVANIA DUTCH AMERICAN FOLK ART, Henry J. Kauffman. 279 photos, 28 drawings of tulipware, Fraktur script, painted tinware, toys, flowered furniture, quilts, samplers, hex signs, house interiors, etc. Full descriptive text. Excellent for tourist, rewarding for designer, collector. Map. 146pp. 7⅞ x 10¾.
                                                21205-X Paperbound $2.50

EARLY NEW ENGLAND GRAVESTONE RUBBINGS, Edmund V. Gillon, Jr. 43 photographs, 226 carefully reproduced rubbings show heavily symbolic, sometimes macabre early gravestones, up to early 19th century. Remarkable early American primitive art, occasionally strikingly beautiful; always powerful. Text. xxvi + 207pp. 8⅜ x 11¼.   21380-3 Paperbound $3.50

ALPHABETS AND ORNAMENTS, Ernst Lehner. Well-known pictorial source for decorative alphabets, script examples, cartouches, frames, decorative title pages, calligraphic initials, borders, similar material. 14th to 19th century, mostly European. Useful in almost any graphic arts designing, varied styles. 750 illustrations. 256pp. 7 x 10.   21905-4 Paperbound $4.00

PAINTING: A CREATIVE APPROACH, Norman Colquhoun. For the beginner simple guide provides an instructive approach to painting: major stumbling blocks for beginner; overcoming them, technical points; paints and pigments; oil painting; watercolor and other media and color. New section on "plastic" paints. Glossary. Formerly *Paint Your Own Pictures*. 221pp.   22000-1 Paperbound $1.75

THE ENJOYMENT AND USE OF COLOR, Walter Sargent. Explanation of the relations between colors themselves and between colors in nature and art, including hundreds of little-known facts about color values, intensities, effects of high and low illumination, complementary colors. Many practical hints for painters, references to great masters. 7 color plates, 29 illustrations. x + 274pp.
20944-X Paperbound $2.75

THE NOTEBOOKS OF LEONARDO DA VINCI, compiled and edited by Jean Paul Richter. 1566 extracts from original manuscripts reveal the full range of Leonardo's versatile genius: all his writings on painting, sculpture, architecture, anatomy, astronomy, geography, topography, physiology, mining, music, etc., in both Italian and English, with 186 plates of manuscript pages and more than 500 additional drawings. Includes studies for the Last Supper, the lost Sforza monument, and other works. Total of xlvii + 866pp. 7⅞ x 10¾.
22572-0, 22573-9 Two volumes, Paperbound $10.00

MONTGOMERY WARD CATALOGUE OF 1895. Tea gowns, yards of flannel and pillow-case lace, stereoscopes, books of gospel hymns, the New Improved Singer Sewing Machine, side saddles, milk skimmers, straight-edged razors, high-button shoes, spittoons, and on and on . . . listing some 25,000 items, practically all illustrated. Essential to the shoppers of the 1890's, it is our truest record of the spirit of the period. Unaltered reprint of Issue No. 57, Spring and Summer 1895. Introduction by Boris Emmet. Innumerable illustrations. xiii + 624pp. 8½ x 11⅝.
22377-9 Paperbound $6.95

THE CRYSTAL PALACE EXHIBITION ILLUSTRATED CATALOGUE (LONDON, 1851). One of the wonders of the modern world—the Crystal Palace Exhibition in which all the nations of the civilized world exhibited their achievements in the arts and sciences—presented in an equally important illustrated catalogue. More than 1700 items pictured with accompanying text—ceramics, textiles, cast-iron work, carpets, pianos, sleds, razors, wall-papers, billiard tables, beehives, silverware and hundreds of other artifacts—represent the focal point of Victorian culture in the Western World. Probably the largest collection of Victorian decorative art ever assembled— indispensable for antiquarians and designers. Unabridged republication of the Art-Journal Catalogue of the Great Exhibition of 1851, with all terminal essays. New introduction by John Gloag, F.S.A. xxxiv + 426pp. 9 x 12.
22503-8 Paperbound $4.50

THE ARCHITECTURE OF COUNTRY HOUSES, Andrew J. Downing. Together with Vaux's *Villas and Cottages* this is the basic book for Hudson River Gothic architecture of the middle Victorian period. Full, sound discussions of general aspects of housing, architecture, style, decoration, furnishing, together with scores of detailed house plans, illustrations of specific buildings, accompanied by full text. Perhaps the most influential single American architectural book. 1850 edition. Introduction by J. Stewart Johnson. 321 figures, 34 architectural designs. xvi + 560pp.

22003-6 Paperbound $4.00

LOST EXAMPLES OF COLONIAL ARCHITECTURE, John Mead Howells. Full-page photographs of buildings that have disappeared or been so altered as to be denatured, including many designed by major early American architects. 245 plates. xvii + 248pp. 7⅞ x 10¾.   21143-6 Paperbound $3.50

DOMESTIC ARCHITECTURE OF THE AMERICAN COLONIES AND OF THE EARLY REPUBLIC, Fiske Kimball. Foremost architect and restorer of Williamsburg and Monticello covers nearly 200 homes between 1620-1825. Architectural details, construction, style features, special fixtures, floor plans, etc. Generally considered finest work in its area. 219 illustrations of houses, doorways, windows, capital mantels. xx + 314pp. 7⅞ x 10¾.   21743-4 Paperbound $4.00

EARLY AMERICAN ROOMS: 1650-1858, edited by Russell Hawes Kettell. Tour of 12 rooms, each representative of a different era in American history and each furnished, decorated, designed and occupied in the style of the era. 72 plans and elevations, 8-page color section, etc., show fabrics, wall papers, arrangements, etc. Full descriptive text. xvii + 200pp. of text. 8⅜ x 11¼.

21633-0 Paperbound $5.00

THE FITZWILLIAM VIRGINAL BOOK, edited by J. Fuller Maitland and W. B. Squire. Full modern printing of famous early 17th-century ms: volume of 300 works by Morley, Byrd, Bull, Gibbons, etc. For piano or other modern keyboard instrument; easy to read format. xxxvi + 938pp. 8⅜ x 11.

21068-5, 21069-3 Two volumes, Paperbound $10.00

KEYBOARD MUSIC, Johann Sebastian Bach. Bach Gesellschaft edition. A rich selection of Bach's masterpieces for the harpsichord: the six English Suites, six French Suites, the six Partitas (Clavierübung part I), the Goldberg Variations (Clavierübung part IV), the fifteen Two-Part Inventions and the fifteen Three-Part Sinfonias. Clearly reproduced on large sheets with ample margins; eminently playable. vi + 312pp. 8⅛ x 11.   22360-4 Paperbound $5.00

THE MUSIC OF BACH: AN INTRODUCTION, Charles Sanford Terry. A fine, nontechnical introduction to Bach's music, both instrumental and vocal. Covers organ music, chamber music, passion music, other types. Analyzes themes, developments, innovations. x + 114pp.   21075-8 Paperbound $1.25

BEETHOVEN AND HIS NINE SYMPHONIES, Sir George Grove. Noted British musicologist provides best history, analysis, commentary on symphonies. Very thorough, rigorously accurate; necessary to both advanced student and amateur music lover. 436 musical passages. vii + 407 pp.   20334-4 Paperbound $2.75

JOHANN SEBASTIAN BACH, Philipp Spitta. One of the great classics of musicology, this definitive analysis of Bach's music (and life) has never been surpassed. Lucid, nontechnical analyses of hundreds of pieces (30 pages devoted to St. Matthew Passion, 26 to B Minor Mass). Also includes major analysis of 18th-century music. 450 musical examples. 40-page musical supplement. Total of xx + 1799pp.
(EUK) 22278-0, 22279-9 Two volumes, Clothbound $15.00

MOZART AND HIS PIANO CONCERTOS, Cuthbert Girdlestone. The only full-length study of an important area of Mozart's creativity. Provides detailed analyses of all 23 concertos, traces inspirational sources. 417 musical examples. Second edition. 509pp. (USO) 21271-8 Paperbound $3.50

THE PERFECT WAGNERITE: A COMMENTARY ON THE NIBLUNG'S RING, George Bernard Shaw. Brilliant and still relevant criticism in remarkable essays on Wagner's Ring cycle, Shaw's ideas on political and social ideology behind the plots, role of Leitmotifs, vocal requisites, etc. Prefaces. xxi + 136pp.
21707-8 Paperbound $1.50

DON GIOVANNI, W. A. Mozart. Complete libretto, modern English translation; biographies of composer and librettist; accounts of early performances and critical reaction. Lavishly illustrated. All the material you need to understand and appreciate this great work. Dover Opera Guide and Libretto Series; translated and introduced by Ellen Bleiler. 92 illustrations. 209pp.
21134-7 Paperbound $1.50

HIGH FIDELITY SYSTEMS: A LAYMAN'S GUIDE, Roy F. Allison. All the basic information you need for setting up your own audio system: high fidelity and stereo record players, tape records, F.M. Connections, adjusting tone arm, cartridge, checking needle alignment, positioning speakers, phasing speakers, adjusting hums, trouble-shooting, maintenance, and similar topics. Enlarged 1965 edition. More than 50 charts, diagrams, photos. iv + 91pp. 21514-8 Paperbound $1.25

REPRODUCTION OF SOUND, Edgar Villchur. Thorough coverage for laymen of high fidelity systems, reproducing systems in general, needles, amplifiers, preamps, loudspeakers, feedback, explaining physical background. "A rare talent for making technicalities vividly comprehensible," R. Darrell, *High Fidelity*. 69 figures. iv + 92pp. 21515-6 Paperbound $1.00

HEAR ME TALKIN' TO YA: THE STORY OF JAZZ AS TOLD BY THE MEN WHO MADE IT, Nat Shapiro and Nat Hentoff. Louis Armstrong, Fats Waller, Jo Jones, Clarence Williams, Billy Holiday, Duke Ellington, Jelly Roll Morton and dozens of other jazz greats tell how it was in Chicago's South Side, New Orleans, depression Harlem and the modern West Coast as jazz was born and grew. xvi + 429pp.
21726-4 Paperbound $2.50

FABLES OF AESOP, translated by Sir Roger L'Estrange. A reproduction of the very rare 1931 Paris edition; a selection of the most interesting fables, together with 50 imaginative drawings by Alexander Calder. v + 128pp. 6½x9¼.
21780-9 Paperbound $1.25

AGAINST THE GRAIN (A REBOURS), Joris K. Huysmans. Filled with weird images, evidences of a bizarre imagination, exotic experiments with hallucinatory drugs, rich tastes and smells and the diversions of its sybarite hero Duc Jean des Esseintes, this classic novel pushed 19th-century literary decadence to its limits. Full unabridged edition. Do not confuse this with abridged editions generally sold. Introduction by Havelock Ellis. xlix + 206pp. 22190-3 Paperbound $2.00

VARIORUM SHAKESPEARE: HAMLET. Edited by Horace H. Furness; a landmark of American scholarship. Exhaustive footnotes and appendices treat all doubtful words and phrases, as well as suggested critical emendations throughout the play's history. First volume contains editor's own text, collated with all Quartos and Folios. Second volume contains full first Quarto, translations of Shakespeare's sources (Belleforest, and Saxo Grammaticus), Der Bestrafte Brudermord, and many essays on critical and historical points of interest by major authorities of past and present. Includes details of staging and costuming over the years. By far the best edition available for serious students of Shakespeare. Total of xx + 905pp.
21004-9, 21005-7, 2 volumes, Paperbound $7.00

A LIFE OF WILLIAM SHAKESPEARE, Sir Sidney Lee. This is the standard life of Shakespeare, summarizing everything known about Shakespeare and his plays. Incredibly rich in material, broad in coverage, clear and judicious, it has served thousands as the best introduction to Shakespeare. 1931 edition. 9 plates. xxix + 792pp. (USO) 21967-4 Paperbound $3.75

MASTERS OF THE DRAMA, John Gassner. Most comprehensive history of the drama in print, covering every tradition from Greeks to modern Europe and America, including India, Far East, etc. Covers more than 800 dramatists, 2000 plays, with biographical material, plot summaries, theatre history, criticism, etc. "Best of its kind in English," New Republic. 77 illustrations. xxii + 890pp.
20100-7 Clothbound $8.50

THE EVOLUTION OF THE ENGLISH LANGUAGE, George McKnight. The growth of English, from the 14th century to the present. Unusual, non-technical account presents basic information in very interesting form: sound shifts, change in grammar and syntax, vocabulary growth, similar topics. Abundantly illustrated with quotations. Formerly Modern English in the Making. xii + 590pp.
21932-1 Paperbound $3.50

AN ETYMOLOGICAL DICTIONARY OF MODERN ENGLISH, Ernest Weekley. Fullest, richest work of its sort, by foremost British lexicographer. Detailed word histories, including many colloquial and archaic words; extensive quotations. Do not confuse this with the Concise Etymological Dictionary, which is much abridged. Total of xxvii + 830pp. 6½ x 9¼.
21873-2, 21874-0 Two volumes, Paperbound $6.00

FLATLAND: A ROMANCE OF MANY DIMENSIONS, E. A. Abbott. Classic of science-fiction explores ramifications of life in a two-dimensional world, and what happens when a three-dimensional being intrudes. Amusing reading, but also useful as introduction to thought about hyperspace. Introduction by Banesh Hoffmann. 16 illustrations. xx + 103pp. 20001-9 Paperbound $1.00

POEMS OF ANNE BRADSTREET, edited with an introduction by Robert Hutchinson. A new selection of poems by America's first poet and perhaps the first significant woman poet in the English language. 48 poems display her development in works of considerable variety—love poems, domestic poems, religious meditations, formal elegies, "quaternions," etc. Notes, bibliography. viii + 222pp.
22160-1 Paperbound $2.00

THREE GOTHIC NOVELS: THE CASTLE OF OTRANTO BY HORACE WALPOLE; VATHEK BY WILLIAM BECKFORD; THE VAMPYRE BY JOHN POLIDORI, WITH FRAGMENT OF A NOVEL BY LORD BYRON, edited by E. F. Bleiler. The first Gothic novel, by Walpole; the finest Oriental tale in English, by Beckford; powerful Romantic supernatural story in versions by Polidori and Byron. All extremely important in history of literature; all still exciting, packed with supernatural thrills, ghosts, haunted castles, magic, etc. xl + 291pp.
21232-7 Paperbound $2.50

THE BEST TALES OF HOFFMANN, E. T. A. Hoffmann. 10 of Hoffmann's most important stories, in modern re-editings of standard translations: Nutcracker and the King of Mice, Signor Formica, Automata, The Sandman, Rath Krespel, The Golden Flowerpot, Master Martin the Cooper, The Mines of Falun, The King's Betrothed, A New Year's Eve Adventure. 7 illustrations by Hoffmann. Edited by E. F. Bleiler. xxxix + 419pp.
21793-0 Paperbound $3.00

GHOST AND HORROR STORIES OF AMBROSE BIERCE, Ambrose Bierce. 23 strikingly modern stories of the horrors latent in the human mind: The Eyes of the Panther, The Damned Thing, An Occurrence at Owl Creek Bridge, An Inhabitant of Carcosa, etc., plus the dream-essay, Visions of the Night. Edited by E. F. Bleiler. xxii + 199pp.
20767-6 Paperbound $1.50

BEST GHOST STORIES OF J. S. LEFANU, J. Sheridan LeFanu. Finest stories by Victorian master often considered greatest supernatural writer of all. Carmilla, Green Tea, The Haunted Baronet, The Familiar, and 12 others. Most never before available in the U. S. A. Edited by E. F. Bleiler. 8 illustrations from Victorian publications. xvii + 467pp.
20415-4 Paperbound $3.00

MATHEMATICAL FOUNDATIONS OF INFORMATION THEORY, A. I. Khinchin. Comprehensive introduction to work of Shannon, McMillan, Feinstein and Khinchin, placing these investigations on a rigorous mathematical basis. Covers entropy concept in probability theory, uniqueness theorem, Shannon's inequality, ergodic sources, the E property, martingale concept, noise, Feinstein's fundamental lemma, Shanon's first and second theorems. Translated by R. A. Silverman and M. D. Friedman. iii + 120pp.
60434-9 Paperbound $1.75

SEVEN SCIENCE FICTION NOVELS, H. G. Wells. The standard collection of the great novels. Complete, unabridged. *First Men in the Moon, Island of Dr. Moreau, War of the Worlds, Food of the Gods, Invisible Man, Time Machine, In the Days of the Comet.* Not only science fiction fans, but every educated person owes it to himself to read these novels. 1015pp.
20264-X Clothbound $5.00

LAST AND FIRST MEN AND STAR MAKER, TWO SCIENCE FICTION NOVELS, Olaf Stapledon. Greatest future histories in science fiction. In the first, human intelligence is the "hero," through strange paths of evolution, interplanetary invasions, incredible technologies, near extinctions and reemergences. Star Maker describes the quest of a band of star rovers for intelligence itself, through time and space: weird inhuman civilizations, crustacean minds, symbiotic worlds, etc. Complete, unabridged. v + 438pp. 21962-3 Paperbound $2.50

THREE PROPHETIC NOVELS, H. G. WELLS. Stages of a consistently planned future for mankind. *When the Sleeper Wakes*, and *A Story of the Days to Come*, anticipate *Brave New World* and *1984*, in the 21st Century; *The Time Machine*, only complete version in print, shows farther future and the end of mankind. All show Wells's greatest gifts as storyteller and novelist. Edited by E. F. Bleiler. x + 335pp. (USO) 20605-X Paperbound $2.50

THE DEVIL'S DICTIONARY, Ambrose Bierce. America's own Oscar Wilde—Ambrose Bierce—offers his barbed iconoclastic wisdom in over 1,000 definitions hailed by H. L. Mencken as "some of the most gorgeous witticisms in the English language." 145pp. 20487-1 Paperbound $1.25

MAX AND MORITZ, Wilhelm Busch. Great children's classic, father of comic strip, of two bad boys, Max and Moritz. Also Ker and Plunk (Plisch und Plumm), Cat and Mouse, Deceitful Henry, Ice-Peter, The Boy and the Pipe, and five other pieces. Original German, with English translation. Edited by H. Arthur Klein; translations by various hands and H. Arthur Klein. vi + 216pp. 20181-3 Paperbound $2.00

PIGS IS PIGS AND OTHER FAVORITES, Ellis Parker Butler. The title story is one of the best humor short stories, as Mike Flannery obfuscates biology and English. Also included, That Pup of Murchison's, The Great American Pie Company, and Perkins of Portland. 14 illustrations. v + 109pp. 21532-6 Paperbound $1.25

THE PETERKIN PAPERS, Lucretia P. Hale. It takes genius to be as stupidly mad as the Peterkins, as they decide to become wise, celebrate the "Fourth," keep a cow, and otherwise strain the resources of the Lady from Philadelphia. Basic book of American humor. 153 illustrations. 219pp. 20794-3 Paperbound $1.50

PERRAULT'S FAIRY TALES, translated by A. E. Johnson and S. R. Littlewood, with 34 full-page illustrations by Gustave Doré. All the original Perrault stories—Cinderella, Sleeping Beauty, Bluebeard, Little Red Riding Hood, Puss in Boots, Tom Thumb, etc.—with their witty verse morals and the magnificent illustrations of Doré. One of the five or six great books of European fairy tales. viii + 117pp. 8⅛ x 11. 22311-6 Paperbound $2.00

OLD HUNGARIAN FAIRY TALES, Baroness Orczy. Favorites translated and adapted by author of the *Scarlet Pimpernel*. Eight fairy tales include "The Suitors of Princess Fire-Fly," "The Twin Hunchbacks," "Mr. Cuttlefish's Love Story," and "The Enchanted Cat." This little volume of magic and adventure will captivate children as it has for generations. 90 drawings by Montagu Barstow. 96pp. (USO) 22293-4 Paperbound $1.95

THE RED FAIRY BOOK, Andrew Lang. Lang's color fairy books have long been children's favorites. This volume includes Rapunzel, Jack and the Bean-stalk and 35 other stories, familiar and unfamiliar. 4 plates, 93 illustrations x + 367pp.
21673-X Paperbound $2.50

THE BLUE FAIRY BOOK, Andrew Lang. Lang's tales come from all countries and all times. Here are 37 tales from Grimm, the Arabian Nights, Greek Mythology, and other fascinating sources. 8 plates, 130 illustrations. xi + 390pp.
21437-0 Paperbound $2.50

HOUSEHOLD STORIES BY THE BROTHERS GRIMM. Classic English-language edition of the well-known tales — Rumpelstiltskin, Snow White, Hansel and Gretel, The Twelve Brothers, Faithful John, Rapunzel, Tom Thumb (52 stories in all). Translated into simple, straightforward English by Lucy Crane. Ornamented with headpieces, vignettes, elaborate decorative initials and a dozen full-page illustrations by Walter Crane. x + 269pp.
21080-4 Paperbound $2.50

THE MERRY ADVENTURES OF ROBIN HOOD, Howard Pyle. The finest modern versions of the traditional ballads and tales about the great English outlaw. Howard Pyle's complete prose version, with every word, every illustration of the first edition. Do not confuse this facsimile of the original (1883) with modern editions that change text or illustrations. 23 plates plus many page decorations. xxii + 296pp.
22043-5 Paperbound $2.50

THE STORY OF KING ARTHUR AND HIS KNIGHTS, Howard Pyle. The finest children's version of the life of King Arthur; brilliantly retold by Pyle, with 48 of his most imaginative illustrations. xviii + 313pp. 6⅛ x 9¼.
21445-1 Paperbound $2.50

THE WONDERFUL WIZARD OF OZ, L. Frank Baum. America's finest children's book in facsimile of first edition with all Denslow illustrations in full color. The edition a child should have. Introduction by Martin Gardner. 23 color plates, scores of drawings. iv + 267pp.
20691-2 Paperbound $2.50

THE MARVELOUS LAND OF OZ, L. Frank Baum. The second Oz book, every bit as imaginative as the Wizard. The hero is a boy named Tip, but the Scarecrow and the Tin Woodman are back, as is the Oz magic. 16 color plates, 120 drawings by John R. Neill. 287pp.
20692-0 Paperbound $2.50

THE MAGICAL MONARCH OF MO, L. Frank Baum. Remarkable adventures in a land even stranger than Oz. The best of Baum's books not in the Oz series. 15 color plates and dozens of drawings by Frank Verbeck. xviii + 237pp.
21892-9 Paperbound $2.25

THE BAD CHILD'S BOOK OF BEASTS, MORE BEASTS FOR WORSE CHILDREN, A MORAL ALPHABET, Hilaire Belloc. Three complete humor classics in one volume. Be kind to the frog, and do not call him names . . . and 28 other whimsical animals. Familiar favorites and some not so well known. Illustrated by Basil Blackwell. 156pp.
(USO) 20749-8 Paperbound $1.50

MATHEMATICAL PUZZLES FOR BEGINNERS AND ENTHUSIASTS, Geoffrey Mott-Smith. 189 puzzles from easy to difficult—involving arithmetic, logic, algebra, properties of digits, probability, etc.—for enjoyment and mental stimulus. Explanation of mathematical principles behind the puzzles. 135 illustrations. viii + 248pp.
20198-8 Paperbound $1.75

PAPER FOLDING FOR BEGINNERS, William D. Murray and Francis J. Rigney. Easiest book on the market, clearest instructions on making interesting, beautiful origami. Sail boats, cups, roosters, frogs that move legs, bonbon boxes, standing birds, etc. 40 projects; more than 275 diagrams and photographs. 94pp.
20713-7 Paperbound $1.00

TRICKS AND GAMES ON THE POOL TABLE, Fred Herrmann. 79 tricks and games— some solitaires, some for two or more players, some competitive games—to entertain you between formal games. Mystifying shots and throws, unusual caroms, tricks involving such props as cork, coins, a hat, etc. Formerly *Fun on the Pool Table*. 77 figures. 95pp.
21814-7 Paperbound $1.00

HAND SHADOWS TO BE THROWN UPON THE WALL: A SERIES OF NOVEL AND AMUSING FIGURES FORMED BY THE HAND, Henry Bursill. Delightful picturebook from great-grandfather's day shows how to make 18 different hand shadows: a bird that flies, duck that quacks, dog that wags his tail, camel, goose, deer, boy, turtle, etc. Only book of its sort. vi + 33pp. 6½ x 9¼. 21779-5 Paperbound $1.00

WHITTLING AND WOODCARVING, E. J. Tangerman. 18th printing of best book on market. "If you can cut a potato you can carve" toys and puzzles, chains, chessmen, caricatures, masks, frames, woodcut blocks, surface patterns, much more. Information on tools, woods, techniques. Also goes into serious wood sculpture from Middle Ages to present, East and West. 464 photos, figures. x + 293pp.
20965-2 Paperbound $2.00

HISTORY OF PHILOSOPHY, Julián Marias. Possibly the clearest, most easily followed, best planned, most useful one-volume history of philosophy on the market; neither skimpy nor overfull. Full details on system of every major philosopher and dozens of less important thinkers from pre-Socratics up to Existentialism and later. Strong on many European figures usually omitted. Has gone through dozens of editions in Europe. 1966 edition, translated by Stanley Appelbaum and Clarence Strowbridge. xviii + 505pp. 21739-6 Paperbound $3.00

YOGA: A SCIENTIFIC EVALUATION, Kovoor T. Behanan. Scientific but non-technical study of physiological results of yoga exercises; done under auspices of Yale U. Relations to Indian thought, to psychoanalysis, etc. 16 photos. xxiii + 270pp.
20505-3 Paperbound $2.50